Thirty Years of Management Briefings
1958 to 1988

Thirty Years

of Management

Briefings

1958 to 1988

IBM Corporation

Armonk, New York

1988

Thirty Years of Management Briefings
1958 to 1988
Published by IBM Corporate Communications

First edition, 1988

To reorder, contact:
Mechanicsburg Distribution Center

Reorder number:
ZZ04-1201

Editor's Note:

These *Management Briefings* capture a great deal of the spirit and substance underlying IBM's management philosophy as it has evolved during the last three decades. A few have been removed because current policy has evolved significantly since they were written nearly two decades ago. There are a number of others, all from that period, that may no longer reflect current policy and practice, or may use outdated language.

For current IBM policy and practice, managers should continue to refer to the *IBM Manager's Manual* and *Business Conduct Guidelines*.

IBM Corporate Communications
February 1988

Foreword

We, in IBM, have consciously built on the best of our past while adapting to meet current challenges. Even with the enormous changes of the last few years, as we worked to transform the IBM company, we have nurtured our heritage.

One of the ways we have preserved and communicated IBM's heritage is through *Management Briefings* – messages from IBM's chief executive officers to all managers. Over the years, briefings have addressed most of the major issues managers face – from good communications to performance evaluations. In this way the cornerstones of IBM management, such as our basic beliefs, have been illuminated and reinforced for successive generations of IBM managers.

This year marks the 30th anniversary of the *Management Briefing* program. Since the briefings provide unique insight into IBM's history and heritage, we have collected the first 30 years of them in this volume. Substituting this book for the old method of producing and distributing previous *Management Briefings* will also save considerable work and money.

Whether you are a new manager or one with years of experience, I think you will find that the heritage reflected here is a source of insight and pride for all of us.

John F. Akers
February 1988

Thomas J. Watson Jr.

Briefings 1-58 through 2-71
1958 – 1971

Thomas J. Watson Jr.

Number 1-58: November 28, 1958

A number of you have expressed a need for more information on company activities, policies and developments. To fill this need we are, with this issue, initiating *Management Briefing*. The basic purpose of this publication is to provide managers throughout the company with more background information about current IBM announcements and activities and explain to the greatest possible degree the "why" behind our policies. In addition, it will contain, from time to time, actual case studies which have an object lesson for the benefit of all management and which can help all of us to do a better job of managing our respective areas of the business.

Management Briefings will be issued whenever important news events occur or policies are formulated which should be reviewed with you. We hope this publication will help you better understand what goes on in the business and to better communicate these activities to the people under your jurisdiction.

Thomas J. Watson Jr.

Number 2-58: November 28, 1958

A department manager in one of our plants, after some hesitation, went to see his project manager on a personal problem – whether to send Christmas cards to people in his department. For years, he had been doing this as a business courtesy. As his responsibility grew, so did his card exchange list. He also made it a practice to greet each member of his department personally before the holiday, which he felt should have been sufficient. He believed the exchange of Christmas cards as a routine business practice put an unnecessary burden of time and money on him.

Although this department manager did not realize it, last year IBM instituted a new procedure on this subject:

The company suggested that no IBMer feel obligated to send business-type cards to anyone else in IBM. The purchase, addressing and mailing of such cards are, of course, not to be charged to the company or handled by secretaries. This new procedure is not intended to prohibit or discourage anyone from sending Christmas cards to other IBMers on a personal basis. It merely states that no one need feel obligated to do so for business reasons.

Object Lesson in Management: Job Reassignments

(The one plus factor in a business error is that it can teach us a lesson. All of us in IBM management can profit from past mistakes, because when analyzing our errors we can better understand the broad management principles involved. From time to time, we will publish object lessons based on actual IBM cases. Places and circumstances will be altered to conceal the identity of individuals.)

An office supervisor in one of the branch offices had not been handling his job satisfactorily for several months. His manager decided to reassign him to another job. However, the man was removed from the position before a new assignment was decided upon.

In the meantime, for over two weeks, the man had the agonizing experience of not knowing what would be his future assignment. Finally he was transferred to a smaller office to handle the same position as originally, on the theory that it would require less responsibility than the job in the larger office.

The result was that the man suffered a double blow to his morale. First, he had been put through the upsetting experience of not having a job for two weeks. Then, although the new office was smaller, the job was essentially the same and he was as unsuccessful in it as in his original position. He soon had to be moved again.

The cause of this problem was the lack of consideration in the humane handling of an individual and a poor evaluation of the man's abilities. Sufficient time was not taken to plan the move so that the office manager was ready with a new job, and one which the man could successfully handle.

Whenever a man is removed from his job because of not fulfilling his responsibilities, a difficult personnel situation is created. These situations at times are made worse by procedures which violate all the good precepts of human relations. If we ever have to reassign a man, we should:

1. Have carefully evaluated his abilities in order to place him in a job which he can handle.
2. Be prepared to offer him a job immediately.

Object Lesson in Management: Broken Promises

Recently we planned to build a new office building in a large city. When it became necessary to request the city to change the zoning restrictions on part of our property, letters were sent to nearby property owners requesting their consent. One of the nearest neighbors and owner of an apartment building immediately adjacent was understandably concerned about the height of that part of the building to adjoin his property line. Our agent wrote a letter to him, reporting what our building plans showed. He was promised that it would be a low structure, the top of which would be below the lower level of his second story apartment windows. The man coordinating the entire building project was not aware of this letter.

In the time that passed during the final planning and early construction, the building plans changed. It happened that the wall adjoining this neighbor's property was raised another story. Unfortunately, our neighbor was never informed. As the structure took shape he addressed the Office of the President stating that IBM had broken its promise to him, and that the resulting change was one of serious injury to the value of his property. Clearly a mistake had been made. Worse, we attempted to negotiate with him rather than to fully acknowledge our error.

The result was that we were obliged to pay a large sum of money to this neighbor because a commitment had been made and not kept. The integrity of the IBM company in the community had been clouded.

This actual case illustrates only too vividly the unhappy and costly results that can be incurred by IBM when a promise is made and broken. As we grow larger and our activities become more diverse and complex, each man must be alert to make no commitments that he is not dead certain will be kept, and when they are made, to assure that they are completely fulfilled. We can eliminate this pitfall by an acknowledgment of personal responsibility for what we say and do, and with a constant regard for the integrity of the individual and of the company.

Thomas J. Watson Jr.

Number 1-59: January 23, 1959

Earlier this month, IBM salesmen who sold 100 percent or more of their 1958 quota met in San Francisco for a three-day Hundred Percent Club convention. Although these conventions have long been an IBM tradition, you, as a manager, may find that some of the many employees who joined us in recent years do not fully understand why we hold these sessions.

Since our company's business starts at the point of sale, more sales mean more opportunities for everyone else in IBM. Anything – such as Hundred Percent conventions – which helps produce good sales results, in effect produces better opportunities for all of us. The conventions help salesmen do a better job by providing:

1. Recognition and reward for each man who meets quota. The conventions have become an integral part of the salesman's incentive system. While other employees receive a salary, the salesman's income, to a large extent, must come from commissions. If he meets quota, he also earns a trip to a convention.

2. A series of meetings to generate year-round sales enthusiasm. A salesman has built-in hazards convincing prospective customers of his ideas. How much he sells is tied in closely with how much sales enthusiasm he can sustain.

3. An opportunity for IBM salesmen from across the country to exchange technical information about systems, applications and sales techniques. New products are announced and demonstrated, and their uses and applications are discussed.

4. An opportunity for salesmen to meet with and hear talks on sales strategy by our top management.

This "Club" idea is not unique to IBM. Years ago, John H. Patterson, President of National Cash Register, was one of the first to establish Hundred Point conventions, as he called them. Thomas J. Watson, one of Patterson's executives, took along the idea when he joined our company in 1914. Today, the technique of sales conventions is used throughout industry.

Thomas J. Watson Jr.

Number 2-59: March 16, 1959

IBM working relationships with other companies, once almost
unheard of, are on the increase. That old "N.I.H." attitude
("If Not Invented Here, it's not worth bothering about") is
being obsoleted by the ever-increasing speed of technological
progress. We simply haven't time to develop and manufacture
everything ourselves. Today we enter into agreements with
other firms – like Texas Instruments Company – to:

- Conserve IBM men, money, facilities.
- Get the benefit of the experience and ingenuity of other
  companies.
- Develop multiple sources of supply.

Our working relationships are negotiated by the Commer-
cial Development Department of the Corporate Staff at the
request of operating divisions. A typical working relationship
provides for joint development, exchange of technical information, patents in specific technical fields. One thing which
is common to all working relationships is that arrangements
should be equally fair and attractive to both companies.
Frequently in the past, IBM has driven for too hard a bargain,
and too often, we have lost out in the long run.

When we enter a working relationship, we multiply our own
effectiveness by teaming up with leading companies whose
specialized experience or facilities can help us. For example,
when we decided to transistorize, we looked for a company
with good semiconductor experience. Texas Instruments had
it, and could produce transistors in quantities we wanted. The
working relationship established late in 1957 provides for exchange of licenses, purchasing arrangements, interchange of
technical information, and joint development of transistors,
as agreed upon from time to time. (We have a similar, not as
broad, agreement with Hughes Aircraft which gives us an
additional source of semiconductors.)

Working relationships like these allow us to concentrate
manpower and facilities on jobs where we excel. Result: more
and better IBM products.

Thomas J. Watson Jr.

Number 3-59: March 20, 1959

There have been a number of problems recently arising from employees believing that credit for their own originality was taken by their superiors.

IBM is getting to be a large company, and while there are many benefits realized by all of us through our continued growth, there is no doubt that as the company increases in size, so does the danger that the individual does not receive recognition for his particular contribution. The success of every manager is dependent upon the success of those working for him. As we grow, each of us must try even harder to give credit where credit is due – to bend over backwards to give recognition to the efforts of every member of our team. No one will carry a chip on his shoulder if he is invited to take a few well deserved bows.

In most areas of the company, the work of individuals can frequently produce a real step forward, whether in technology, improved manufacturing ideas, or better customer service. One of the basic incentives and principal rewards is recognition and it is important that they receive it.

Because of the complex nature of our business, it sometimes seems impossible to give complete credit for every suggestion or new idea which is given to one. When it is not possible for a manager to recognize individually the contributions of his subordinates, a great deal can be accomplished by bringing the team together at frequent intervals and stating simply, but forcefully, the fine contributions the team is making to the success of the department.

One of the most important duties of a manager is to be sensitive to the needs of those who work for him. Giving credit where it is due is absolutely essential to building high morale and will do much to add strength to the IBM company.

Thomas J. Watson Jr.

Number 4-59: July 6, 1959

Poor handling of "problem employees" can backfire on you.
Here's an object lesson on how not to handle it:

A secretary in one of our branch offices resigned after two
years with IBM, charging that she'd been humiliated and un-
fairly treated. Investigation showed her charges were partially
true. She had been under a doctor's care during most of her
IBM career, had frequently been absent, but always for legitimate medical reasons. These absences, and her poor health,
made it almost impossible for her to be of much service to IBM.
This was apparent almost from the day she joined IBM.

Her office manager failed to get at the heart of the problem
and instead spent nearly two years bickering with her about her
absences and accusing her of faking illness. Finally, in a fit of
rage, he told her he was "not running a rest home for invalids."
In that mood, he called her in for her semi-annual appraisal.
He appraised her as a very poor employee in every respect.

Next day she told him she was resigning. During this interview she broke down and cried. He quickly reversed his appraisal, tried to talk her into staying. When she refused, he
called her husband on the phone, advised him to get her to a
psychiatrist because she was suffering from some grave emotional problem. Her husband left his work to take her home.
She stuck by her resolution to resign, and left with considerable bitterness toward IBM.

The mistakes of the office manager are clear. These lessons
are equally clear:

- Don't let a personnel problem linger. Get the facts and
  discuss them frankly with the employee, making sure that
  you reach an understanding and plan a mutually satisfactory solution.
- Try not to involve employees' families in their job problems.
- If medical, psychiatric, legal or spiritual advice is called for,
  let it be given by someone competent in that field.
- It's possible to be firm and tactful at the same time.

Thomas J. Watson Jr.

Number 5-59: September 4, 1959

Many of us occasionally feel the need to speak forth publicly on controversial matters. But some of us, I know, hesitate to speak up sometimes for fear that what we say will reflect adversely on our company. I thought it might be helpful to tell you my beliefs on this matter. Three principles are involved:

First – We ask no one, simply because he works for IBM, to modify his opinions or strain his beliefs to suit our business. We certainly respect every employee's right to believe what he chooses.

Second – It is essential that anyone who accepts an IBM managerial responsibility believe in the basic objectives of that responsibility. Anything less would not permit a person to do a good job. It would be unfair to the individual and to IBM.

Third – We cannot say anything deliberately to hurt or embarrass our customers, for they have given us their confidence.

If an assignment is incompatible with a manager's basic beliefs, he should not accept it. It follows, then, when there is no conflict between a manager's basic beliefs and his job responsibilities, he will not be faced with the problem of opposing his business interests when he speaks publicly about things in which he believes.

Voicing constructive opinions on matters important to our communities and country is essential to good citizenship. So, I am delighted when IBMers offer thoughtful opinions on such matters. Many of us do this now. I think we must keep it up.

Thomas J. Watson Jr.

Number 6-59: October 29, 1959

Failure to delegate is the biggest single obstacle to job performance in IBM. That's the opinion of a representative group of IBM's middle management who took part in an Opinion Research Corporation study of twelve major U.S. corporations.

ORC was trying to find out if "conformity" is as big a problem in large corporations as it's cracked up to be. Here's what they found out:

- The man most likely to succeed in a corporation is not the conformist – the organization man – but the man of initiative who crashes through to get things done in spite of risks and obstacles.
- It's not conformity that keeps a good man down, but "administrative excesses" – sometimes called "bureaucracy."
- IBM managers apparently chafe under these "excesses" more than managers in the other companies taking part in the study.

Although failure of superiors to delegate was the complaint most often cited by the IBM managers (47 percent cited this as an obstacle to job performance), they complained of other obstacles too, all of which seem to be related to lack of delegation:

- Lack of planning, too many crash projects, lack of long-range goals, short-range jobs interfering with long-range goals.
- Delayed decisions from above, too much "base touching" and collective decision making.
- Difficulty in getting information from higher up and difficulty in reaching higher levels of management for exchange of ideas.
- Too many minor matters interfering with important projects.

The IBM managers who took part in this study differed from the managers in the other companies in that they: were younger, had less managerial experience, were promoted faster, are more eager for responsibility, are not afraid of conflict, like their work and work harder, put in longer hours, and work for a company that is growing faster and has recently been decentralized. Those might be some of the reasons they tend to "chafe" more under administrative excesses.

But this does not mean that these administrative obstacles are not a serious problem in IBM. Just how serious, we don't know. The managers who took part in this study were representative of "middle" management. But we can assume that the obstacles they complained about do exist – to some extent – at all levels.

What can we do about it? Certainly these "administrative excesses" are not the result of any conscious planning. To a certain extent they're inevitable in any organization. They develop out of the pressures of day-to-day work. For that reason, they can't be stamped out by an announcement from 590 Madison Avenue that "henceforth all administrative excesses will cease." They can never be utterly stamped out, but they can be held within reasonable limits if we each study our own work attitudes and habits and make sure that we ourselves are not guilty of creating for others the same obstacles we complain of.

Perhaps it would help if each of us reviewed these findings with our subordinates, asking, "Are these administrative obstacles present in our operation? If so, why? What can we do to overcome them?"

Another interesting part of the ORC study was the answers IBM managers gave to one of the questions included in the survey:

"If an ambitious young man asked your advice on what he has to do to get ahead in management in your company, what would you tell him, aside from hard work?"

Here are some of their answers:

– "Develop a passion for doing the assignment better and

differently than similar assignments were done before."
- "Be prepared to fail occasionally and to profit by it."
- "Make an honest 'self-inventory' of your abilities. Then capitalize on the things you do best. Don't try to be all things to all people – but confidently push in the areas where you excel. Demonstrate your ability to create without guidance in those areas."
- "Be more concerned with the job you are doing than with the job you expect."
- "Make decisions as you see them and not as you think your boss will like them."

Thomas J. Watson Jr.

Number 7-59: December 8, 1959

Here's a reminder on accepting Christmas gifts from vendors: don't.

We can deal fairly with each of our 14,000 vendors only if we remain free the year round to choose them on their own merits. For any IBMer – whether he deals with vendors or not – to accept a gift from any outside firm or firm's representative might put us under obligation to that firm. Therefore, every year, a few weeks before Christmas, a letter is sent to each vendor, thanking him for his cooperation and explaining our practice.

If you do receive a gift from a vendor, or from anyone who is trying to sell us goods or services, here's what to do: return it to the vendor with a letter acknowledging it and explaining our practice. Perishable items should be given to a local hospital, institution or charitable organization, and a letter sent to the vendor, acknowledging the gift, explaining our practice, and telling him where it was sent. Items classed as advertising novelties (like calendars, ashtrays or pens, with vendor advertising on them) may be kept.

Object Lesson: We Are All Recruiters

Recruiting the best people we can find is a job for all of us. Our professional recruiting people are on the job all the time, of course, but unless we each make the personnel needs of IBM a personal concern, we can lose valuable people. Here's a case in which we almost did.

A young lady, recently graduated with an excellent record from a top engineering school, was interviewed at one of our plants. The interviewer recognized her capabilities, but there was no suitable opening at that plant. He told her IBM had nothing for her. A few weeks later, back in her home town, she related her story to an IBM friend, who was with the local branch office. This IBMer referred her to his branch manager who interviewed and hired her for systems service work. She is now becoming a first-rate systems service representative.

The specific object lesson here is that we should not forget there are plenty of well-educated women today with excellent qualifications for jobs in IBM. Don't overlook them.

Another lesson is that, when interviewing applicants, we shouldn't limit our sights to our own department's needs. If you can't use an applicant who seems to be of top calibre, be sure to give the rest of the company a chance. If you're in a branch office, refer the applicant to your district. If you're in a plant, laboratory, or divisional or corporate headquarters, refer him to your personnel people.

We simply can't afford to pass up any outstanding applicant until we've exhausted every possibility of using his capabilities somewhere in IBM. Let's not lose good people by default.

Thomas J. Watson Jr.

Number 1-60: February 2, 1960

Object Lesson in Management: Are We Too Smug?

One of our salesmen was ushered into a company president's office one morning not long ago. It was his first day on quota. He was full of confidence. As he shot out his hand, he announced, with all the conviction he could muster, "I'm from IBM." Apparently, he had mustered a little too much conviction. The president, not at all impressed by this remarkable disclosure, replied blandly, "What do you want, a medal?"

About a month ago, an IBMer was present at a convention of academic people, most of whom use our equipment in their work. One academician, while talking with this IBMer, mentioned he thought IBM people were "entirely too smug."

A year ago at another convention, a scientist who had worked with IBMers many times complained to an IBM employee that IBMers are "much more complacent and self-satisfied than they should be."

These may be isolated instances – or expressions of a widespread impression we might sometimes create. None of us probably would regard our company as a "smug outfit." But IBM can be hurt just as much if other people think we are smug.

Because we are a leader in our industry, people are apt to be somewhat sensitive to our corporate and individual behavior. Even just a little too much pride can easily be regarded as "smugness." We should all be aware of this, and guard against it. Self-satisfaction – or even its appearance – is just about the weakest posture for any company, or any individual in the company.

We are certainly entitled to a healthy confidence. But in our dealings with customers, vendors, the press, neighbors in the community, we should never exaggerate IBM's capabilities, make light of our competitors, or promise more than we can do. Above all, we should never flaunt our company's growth or our personal success in IBM.

Thomas J. Watson Jr.

Number 2-60: March 23, 1960

Object Lesson: Employee Orientation

Because IBM employees get information about the company in many ways – employee newspapers, booklets, meetings, orientation lectures – we sometimes just assume they know everything we expect of them, and everything they can expect from IBM. Managers can't afford this assumption.

Case in point: The wife of an employee at one of our laboratories was ill during the almost two years her husband had been working for IBM. A chronic illness kept her hospitalized a great deal and required expensive treatment. Throughout this time, she and her husband were unaware that she was automatically covered by the IBM Family Major Medical Plan. They finally learned this fact from an IBM neighbor. The husband's manager had assumed the man knew all about his benefits.

Fortunately in this case, something could be done to remedy the manager's oversight. The employee was paid several thousand dollars under the plan. A manager's oversight in an area like safety, for instance, might not be so easily remedied.

The lesson: It's your responsibility to see that the orientation of any employee reporting to you is complete and up-to-date. No matter what you may think he knows, you should be certain he knows the following:

- *His job.* His department's function, how it relates to the total company effort, and what is specifically expected of him in performance.
- *His pay.* How much, when and how he is paid, the IBM merit pay system, shift premiums, overtime pay, payroll deductions, benefits and how to apply for them.
- *Rules.* Work and shift schedules, lunch periods, regulations on overtime, time cards, absences and tardiness, safety rules, security rules, location and proper use of first aid and safety facilities.

These points are merely a suggested outline. A complete check list is available in the *Manager's Manual.*

Thomas J. Watson Jr.

Number 3-60: April 1, 1960

During the Hundred Percent Club, I had an opportunity to make a few remarks about what can, and often does, happen to organizations when they become as large and as complex as the IBM company. Because this affects each of us personally and because the path we follow as a company will be determined by our individual actions, I want to bring it to the attention of all managers.

Either we are going to maintain our vigor and continue to grow, or we are going to lapse into a pattern of bureaucracy, become slow moving, and eventually stagnate.

Several instances have come to my attention recently of a practice that will work against our keeping our company going in the right direction – this is the practice of "playing it safe." It appears in many forms – from excessive copying of people in correspondence to committees organized not for thoughtful deliberation but to share responsibility.

Even more serious than the resulting waste and lost opportunities is the effect this practice has on those who look to us as examples. We go to great lengths to bring people into IBM who have the potential for developing into strong leaders capable of positive decisions based on sound judgment and firm conviction. The manager who sets the example of "playing it safe" is destructive of our most valuable human asset.

Each of us must be alert to the dangers inherent in practices such as "playing it safe" and act courageously based on what he believes is right. This will assure our company continuing as a dynamic growing organization.

Thomas J. Watson Jr.

Number 4-60: June 10, 1960

Object Lesson: The Man Who Grew a Beard

If all the folklore about our alleged conformity, starched collars, blue suits and song books were collected, it would fill a fair-sized book. We can take a joke, surely. But when folklore comes to life, as it recently did in one of our locations, it is time to take a hard look at the petty social disciplines some managers apparently are still enforcing.

A young man hired as an accounting machine operator decided to grow a beard. The first day he came to work after this decision, his manager told him to get a shave. During several conferences, the manager attempted to persuade him to shave off his beard. He told him that his appearance did not fit in with the decor or with IBM's corporate image.

When the employee steadfastly refused to remove his beard, he was asked if he wished to resign. He replied by asking if IBM wished to fire him. He was fired. When the case was reviewed by higher management, he was offered his job back. But he refused and is now employed elsewhere.

You might be able to make out a good case for discouraging beards under certain circumstances. But there's no case whatever for the way this incident was handled. The corporate design program applies to things like products, buildings, publications and interior decor. Not to people.

Obviously we want high standards of behavior and grooming in this organization. But such standards should be general, not specific. The object is to make sure we are always able to represent the IBM company in the best possible way. Not that we should all look alike, or be walking, talking replicas of our superiors. Let's not confuse propriety with uniformity.

Thomas J. Watson Jr.

Number 5-60: July 29, 1960

Background Briefing: Your Basic Management Responsibilities

Reprinted below are the basic responsibilities of IBM managers. They may seem pretty self-evident to you, but self-evident things have a way of fading out of focus if they're not referred to occasionally. That's why it's necessary to get down on paper the basic ideas that guide a corporation, even when they seem obvious. Statements like this serve as check points of our performance, because these general responsibilities underlie all our specific responsibilities. It might be a good idea to occasionally give yourself a quick test to see how well you carry out these responsibilities. Certainly they should be reviewed with new managers.

Every member of management is expected and required, as an essential part of his responsibilities, to promote the interests of IBM as a whole, to conduct his activities within the framework of corporate policies, and to facilitate the work of other IBM units which his actions affect.

The following responsibilities apply in varying degrees to all management positions.

1. Develop and recommend long- and short-range objectives, policies and plans designed to produce the most profitable results attainable from his assigned area.
2. Understand and comply with established corporate policies, procedures and instructions and ensure that subordinates do likewise; recommend changes when it appears that existing policy is no longer appropriate; direct day-to-day operations of his organization to attain established objectives.
3. Submit realistic budgets, as required, reflecting the anticipated income and/or expenditures of his activity; administer his activity within approved budgets.
4. Detect the need for and propose modifications in plans and operating methods which will result in improvements.

5. Staff his organization with capable people; train sub-ordinates in the competent performance of their duties; periodically appraise their performance and develop suitable replacements, including a successor for himself.

6. Assign responsibility clearly so that subordinates know what they are expected to do, the extent of their authority, and the standards by which they will be judged; provide adequate guidance, counsel and supervision but give them sufficient authority to carry out their assignments and make decisions.

7. Create an atmosphere conducive to management development by encouragement and praise for initiative, imagination and resourcefulness, and by advice and example in the exercise of judgment.

8. Coordinate the activities of organizational units under his supervision to ensure performance on an integrated basis.

9. Keep informed of developments affecting his products, service or area of specialization and to the extent possible, utilize these to the benefit of IBM.

10. Institute adequate safety measures in the work areas under his control through elimination of potential hazards and safety education of subordinates in work practices and use of equipment.

11. Cooperate actively with his associates, both line and staff, to further the attainment of IBM's objectives.

12. Establish and maintain regular two-way communications with all of his employees on policies, procedures or changes; hold regular meetings with his people; keep them informed and give them an opportunity to bring up matters which concern them; be a good source of information about IBM and a good listener when employees come to him with questions, problems or ideas.

Thomas J. Watson Jr.

Number 6-60: August 8, 1960

A disturbing series of events has been coming to my attention and it seems necessary that I review these with you and ask for your cooperation in bringing about an improved situation. The events all pertain to inside trading in the stocks of companies doing business with IBM.

This business has operated on the very highest ethical principles throughout its history and it would be sad indeed, if, as a management, we were unable to continue to maintain this reputation for integrity just because we have grown. The facts, however, indicate that some of us in the company are not adhering to these high principles, probably through misunderstanding, and I think all managers must be cognizant of the problem and must work towards its solution.

As we have become a great corporation, our influence upon the success or failure of smaller companies from which we purchase becomes very great indeed. It has come to my attention that the stock value of a number of companies has increased materially on the information that IBM was intending to purchase their goods or, in fact, had contracted to do so. The brokerage offices in the towns where we have large facilities have been busy taking orders from IBMers who were purchasing stocks in these corporations based on inside knowledge of IBM's intentions to do business with them. These brokerage representatives have then contacted their New York offices and, based on IBMers' purchases, other purchases have been recommended to and made by outsiders.

Obviously, when the stock of a small company is raised in value substantially on a rumor that IBM is going to do business with it, lots of people can be hurt and, if the rumor comes from IBM – either by word of mouth or by purchase of stock by IBM personnel – the operation in mind is highly unethical.

It would not be fair or right to make a rule that no IBMer could own stock in a company with which IBM is doing business. Obviously, IBMers in a purchasing position to influence contractual terms or quantities are specifically barred from trading in the stocks of these organizations. I am sure, however, that each person, if he is being completely honest with himself, knows whether or not he is operating on inside information – or enabling others to do so. This individual appraisal is the acid test. We do not want to get the reputation of having a large number of people who are more interested in the stock market than in their jobs, and yet, corridor talks in certain IBM areas are concentrated to an astonishing degree on that subject.

I hope none of you will overinterpret this memorandum. It is not sent with the idea of condemning anyone, but simply to alert all of you to a situation which is going on and which, if allowed to continue, could seriously damage our reputation and weaken us, thus reducing the future opportunities of each of us.

Thomas J. Watson Jr.

Number 7-60: September 30, 1960

Object Lesson: "Passing the Buck" with Inadequate Employees

Nobody likes to fire a person, even if he – or she – is obviously inadequate. But it's a task most managers have to face up to sooner or later, although often the tendency is to pass the buck and let the next manager do it. Here's an Object Lesson with a hero in it: A manager who recognized the problem, faced up to it, and solved it.

A woman at one of our plants had been hired some five years ago. Since then, she was transferred several times and all reports on her indicated she was performing satisfactorily. Actually, she had been inadequate from the beginning, but none of her managers was willing to tell her, or to help her do better, or to recommend she be discharged.

This game of buck-passing ended abruptly when she was transferred to a young, alert manager who immediately realized she was a substandard employee. He notified his management and the plant Personnel Department. Together they worked out a program of weekly counseling to help the woman improve. The woman was told that she would be dismissed if she failed to improve. She did not improve. Her tasks were elementary, and ones she certainly should have been able to perform satisfactorily. After two months, she was released.

We hear that managers are often afraid their action will be reversed if the employee appeals through the Open Door policy. If a manager makes his decision after sound counseling of the employee, based on honest and thoughtful evaluation, and after he has made every effort to help the employee improve, he should certainly not worry about having to defend it. Actually, only in rare instances has a manager's decision in such matters been reversed. And then, only when the manager has failed in his first obligation: to give the employee every possible opportunity to help himself.

It hurts the company and the employee when a weak manager doesn't give an honest evaluation of an employee's performance. The quicker such problems are identified and solved, the better. The last thing we want to do is be harsh or hasty in our judgments, but the worst thing you can do is let an employee continue on at a substandard level, deceiving himself and the company. The best thing you can do is give him a frank evaluation, suggest ways to improve his performance and counsel him frequently. This way, if he does not improve, there will be no question about the fairness of your decision.

Thomas J. Watson Jr.

Number 1-61: March 16, 1961

Many things are responsible for the success of IBM, and we can profit by taking a fresh look at these things once in a while. One of the things my father always tried to impress me with was that the success we want as individuals and as a business is the kind that is built and sustained by the good will of other people. None of us wants any other kind of success, even though it might sometimes seem tempting to take the short cut.

The only way we can be sure of keeping this good will is always to consider the total impact of our personal and collective behavior. The little things we do – or fail to do – often testify louder than the loudest statements of our intentions. It is easy to be big in big things, in big moments, when everyone is watching. Real character emerges in the way we meet our routine, everyday obligations.

I am tempted to call this simply "salesmanship," but it is of a higher order than that. It means that if we want to have an excellent reputation, we have to be excellent – in everything.

Let me bring this out of the clouds and down to specifics. Really big people are, above everything, courteous, considerate, and generous, not just to some people, in some circumstances, but to everyone all the time. One of the reasons we are known as a great company is that we are known as a company made up of people like that. Let me give you three examples of what I'm talking about. I'm sure we can all think of examples that are equally applicable from our own experience.

Many of us will commit discourtesies over the telephone we would never think of doing face-to-face. Nothing, to my mind, is more discourteous than to have your secretary place a call to someone and then not be available when the call goes through. You can imagine what your reaction would be to a salesman who placed a call to you and then kept you waiting ten minutes after you'd picked up your phone. (While we're on the subject, we again ought to resolve always to answer our own phones, as far as that is possible.)

Again, many of us use manners in our offices I am sure we would never use in our homes. Which of us would greet a visitor in our home seated in an easy chair, and then permit the visitor to leave unescorted to the door?

Consideration, to me, means simply taking into account the pressures, the problems, the commitments of the other person. The manager who calls someone to his office for a fifteen minute conference, and keeps him an hour and a half while he answers several phone calls and takes care of a few other minor matters, is certainly not considering that his visitor has a job of his own to get done.

I mentioned generosity as one of the things we have to practice as individuals if, as a company, we want to keep the reputation we have earned. Generosity does not mean being an "easy touch." It is being generous with our time, our talent, our attention, whenever we have an opportunity to be of service to one another, or to outsiders. This means doing what we are expected to do, and then some. That little extra time and attention can make all the difference in the world to a customer, as any good salesman or customer engineer or office person knows. Inside the company, I can think of nothing that could cause us to deteriorate faster than the spread of the attitude of doing just what we have to do, and not a jot more.

Perhaps I just notice it more lately, but it seems to me that everywhere I turn these days there is less courtesy, less consideration, less genuine desire to be of service. If this is indeed a trend in our society, and not just my imagination, I hope IBM will swim against it.

Thomas J. Watson Jr.

Number 2-61: March 27, 1961

We are a big company now, but I hope we haven't grown so big that individual managers no longer feel responsible for the total success of the company. With our decentralization, it's very easy to become so concerned with our own immediate responsibility, that we may forget we are all working for the IBM company.

Bureaucracy is not something that grows only in government bureaus. It can grow in any organization, large or small, if we lose sight of the fact that individual success and corporate success are inseparable.

Within the last few days, I have talked with two important people anxious to do business with us. These people had been to an embarrassingly large number of places in our company – with no action – before coming to see me. One of them had talked to 18 different IBMers in an attempt to get the answer to a quite simple question. In either case, these men could have been directed to the right person at their first inquiry if the man they approached had simply picked up the telephone and found out who had the information they wanted.

The man cooling his heels outside your office may not look important to you, but this is no reason for not giving him a full, attentive and courteous hearing. Anyone calling on the IBM company should be treated as if he were the most important caller in the world. He might well be prepared to offer the IBM company something that could make him the most important caller in the world, as far as we are concerned. As we get bigger and more successful, it's easy to feel that we don't need the advice or services of outsiders anymore. Let me assure you that nothing could be further from the truth.

It is the business of each of us approached by an outsider to make certain the caller is given the courtesy he deserves and referred to the right person. If you are not the right person, please make sure that whomever you refer the caller to is the person who can give him a full and adequate answer. We have not grown so big, and we are not so successful, that we no longer need the help of others. Nor are we so securely on top that we can all lean back in our chairs and lull ourselves into thinking IBM will go on forever, whatever we, as individuals, do or don't do.

Thomas J. Watson Jr.

"Why worry about 'cost reduction' when we have a good
earnings picture?"

That's a question many employees may have asked you.
Certainly, some of them have thought of it.

To answer it properly, you have to consider our competition
and how we can best meet it. As you know, our competition
is getting stiffer all the time. Just ten years ago we had only a
handful of competitors, all smaller than we. Today, we have
well over 100 competitors, including some of the country's
largest corporations. The best way to meet this competition is
to keep our prices competitive. Prices involve costs and earnings. To understand why we need to watch costs, let's define
costs and earnings.

Costs?

They are what it takes just to stay in business. They include: our
salaries, benefits, equipment, materials, services, taxes, interest
on loans and many other operating expenses. We need constantly to spend large sums in research and development of
new products which will not produce revenue for some years to
come. Without funds for this vital expense, competition would
eventually surpass IBM.

Earnings?

They are what's left over after all costs and expenses are met.
How are they used? In three ways:

– We must pay for new tools, plants, laboratories, offices and
  other facilities needed to keep up with our expanding
  markets.
– Our data processing products require heavy investments.
  Since much of this equipment is rented rather than sold,
  it takes time for these investments to pay off.

— We need to pay a return to our stockholders for their investment.

Clearly, earnings are essential to our future if we are to continue to be a growth company – that is, an expanding one. It's important to all employees that IBM remain a growth company. Growth means greater opportunities for employees.

Growth also requires capital investment in our business. While earnings are higher, so is the capital invested. For example, in the last ten years we added $1,150 million to our invested capital. Of this total, we increased our debt $340 million; we reinvested in the business $550 million of our earnings; and we sold approximately $260 million worth of stock (including the $226 million common stock financing in 1957 and the subsequent sale of stock to employees). In obtaining a fair return on our increasing capital, our earnings must also grow to keep pace with our increased capital invested.

Summing up: Despite our good earnings picture, we will continue to need cost control and reduction. To meet our growing competition, we must continue to offer our products at competitive prices. Since earnings are vital to continued growth, we must continue our cost control. Competition is concentrating on their costs and if we don't, we will eventually be out of business.

Press Relations: Your Role

Few companies in the world today have greater day-to-day involvement with the working press than does IBM. The technological advances of our products, the growth of our industry and IBM's size and geographical scope, have made us a focal point of press attention.

Over the years IBM has enjoyed good relations with the press, and by and large we have been treated fairly. But helping to make this favorable and accurate coverage continue is an increasingly complex job. The IBMers responsible for releasing material to the press and for answering questions from reporters are in the Department of Information. In every one of our divisions and subsidiary headquarters, and in almost all our plants and laboratories, as well as at CHQ, there is an Information or Communications Department. Press relations is its job. But because every manager may find himself dealing with a reporter, you should know the ground rules for working with the press.

A reporter, for example, may call you directly or approach you at a public meeting. When you speak to him you become an IBM spokesman, and your words could conceivably be flashed around the country or the world by a news service.

There is no substitute for your own good judgment in this type of situation, but here are some guidelines:

- Unless you are sure you are completely within your area of authority and certain of the facts, either limit your comments or don't comment at all, explaining it would be inappropriate to do so.
- Get the reporter's name and affiliation, and his deadline, and tell him he will be contacted by the proper person.
- Refer the request to the Information people at your location or division. It's important that the press gets a *prompt* answer.
- Before you do give information to the press, be sure to consider the following:

  - Does the information concern confidential, proprietary or classified subject matter?
  - Are you certain the information is correct, current and consistent with IBM's position on this subject?
  - Has the information been previously released officially?
  - Would the release of such information be harmful to IBM or its people?

- Does the information concern customers, suppliers
  or other individuals or companies from whom clearance
  should be obtained?

- Notify your Information Department after any such press
  contact.
- If you see an erroneous statement about IBM in the press,
  inform your Information people promptly, so they can take
  any action that is necessary.

Thomas J. Watson Jr.

Number 4-61: May 31, 1961

As a manager, you'll probably spend over three-quarters of your time at work today communicating.

Actually, according to an industry-wide study, management people spend about that amount of time talking, listening, writing – to communicate the information necessary to conduct their business and motivate their people. Since communication is a big part of managing and because our opinion surveys have shown that your employees consider you their preferred source of information, we recently conducted a study of how IBM managers communicate.

We asked an outside research firm to administer questionnaires and conduct in-depth interviews with a representative group of our managers. These managers were asked how they received information on IBM policies and procedures, how they rated their communication sources, and how they in turn passed information on to their people. What we learned may be helpful to you in your day-to-day work of communicating with other managers and with employees:

First – Managers at every level say there should be more emphasis on face-to-face communications with opportunity for discussion and questions. When it comes to information on "what is really going on at IBM," they want to get it verbally from their own bosses, from meetings, or from informal discussions. About 80% of the managers said they would rather hear about an important new policy directly from their bosses than in any other form. This makes sense because in face-to-face communications you can ask questions if you don't understand. You can't question a sheet of paper.

Second – IBM managers say it's easy to over-communicate if your messages are too many and too long. Then the receiver has to plow through wordage and often misses the key part. When a written message is needed, we should always consider the recipient's needs – what he must know. We should highlight the important points in the first part of the memo or letter – not bury them in the middle. We could all be less wordy, less complicated, more sharply focused in our writing.

Third – The individuals in our study pointed out that their own managers don't always remember to give reasons – explain the background – for new procedures or instructions. No request, directive or policy can be considered really well communicated unless the people you've told about it know what's behind it – why it's necessary. If you want a man to do the whole job, you have to give him the whole story.

To sum up: No one expects you to be a perfect communicator. But in communicating with managers or employees you might want to try making better use of face-to-face methods, improving and simplifying your written messages, and remembering to explain the "why" of any policy or procedure you pass on to your people.

Feedback Sensitivity: An Object Lesson With a Hero

Most of us are so used to thinking of personnel problems in terms of substandard employees we might forget that above-standard people can cause problems too – if we're insensitive to the special problems, we may cause them. Here's a case where a manager was sensitive enough to spot some feedback signs. As a result, he saw that there was more than met the eye in an employee's dissatisfaction.

A man who had been hired as a toolmaker at one of our plants decided one day, after only four months with IBM, that he wanted to resign immediately. Asked why, he said he simply didn't enjoy working for IBM and preferred to work at his old job in a local machine shop. His old employer had offered his job back without any loss of seniority. Since the toolmaker had been with us such a short time, the easiest thing might have been simply to bid him adieu. The result would have been a good man lost and a disgruntled ex-IBMer in the community telling people that we were not worth working for.

At this point, a sensitive manager got into the act. He was managing the department while the man's immediate manager was away on a special assignment. He was not satisfied to lose a good employee that easily. He was inquisitive enough to probe beneath the surface to find out why the man really wanted to leave. He and the toolmaker sat down and talked. Here's what the manager learned:

The man was a craftsman. He enjoyed, and had pride in, his craft. He had made several good suggestions for improving the plant operations. None had been acted upon. He felt we were not really interested in having a first-class operation and he was not interested in working anywhere else. He felt he was slightly underpaid in comparison with the people with whom he worked.

The manager did two things. He explained that management was highly pleased with the employee and that further demonstration of his excellent work would result in a continued assessment of his capabilities to be sure he was being paid what he was worth. The employee was then invited – if he would change his mind about leaving – to take the rest of the day off and put his ideas about the plant on paper.

Result: the toolmaker was satisfied, felt that his value was appreciated and decided to stay.

Thomas J. Watson Jr.

Number 5-61: June 12, 1961

The article printed on the following pages is appearing in the next *Business Machines*. It covers conflict of interest and ethical conduct. Why it's being sent out is explained in the article. Also, the article suggests that employees contact their managers if they have any questions.

A policy like this necessarily must be stated broadly. It's simply impossible to lay down the solution for every situation. So, you should make it clear to your people that on this policy – as with all policies – you are available for advice on any problems concerning it. You might further point out that if you can't answer an employee's question, you will get the answer for him. Here are some general guides for you:

– There are several practices covered by this policy which are clearly prohibited (as outlined in *Business Machines*) and on which you can give a firm ruling if a question arises:

  Suppliers. Certainly you can determine if an employee is in a position to influence IBM's decisions with respect to any particular IBM supplier. If this is the case, it is quite clear that the employee can own no financial interests in or hold any position with that supplier.

  Gifts and entertainment. In most cases, it certainly should be clear what constitutes "extended entertainment," "expensive gifts," or "unusual favors."

  Mutual funds. No employee – the policy states clearly – should be an officer of a mutual fund.

  Inside information. The use of such information by an employee for personal gain, or to enable others to make such gains, is flatly prohibited.

– In any case, if you aren't sure of the answer, you should contact the person designated for interpretation of this policy in your area of the business.

– Obviously, the best thing you can do is familiarize yourself completely with the policy so you can follow it in letter and spirit, and be able to help answer any of your people's questions.

Reprinted from *Business Machines*, Volume 44, Issue 5, 1961

Good business ethics cannot be too strongly emphasized. Here is IBM's position on this matter.

Recently, many people in IBM received a memorandum from the company on business ethics. It was sent only to those in IBM who have the most contact with suppliers or otherwise would be most apt to find themselves in a conflict of interest or similar situation where the question of proper business ethics might arise.

Most IBMers are not likely to be involved in such situations. However, because it is possible that anyone could be, it is a good idea for every employee to be generally familiar with the company's position.

The company believes that a high standard of business ethics is of critical importance in our society. We have always followed the highest ethical principles and have achieved a reputation for doing so. To maintain that reputation, each employee must observe the highest standards of business integrity and avoid any activity which might tend to embarrass IBM or him. So that every employee will have an opportunity to become familiar with the company's position, the text of the memorandum is presented below.

After reading the memorandum, if you have questions, please get in touch with your immediate manager. He will give you an answer or put you in contact with others who can.

Conflicts of Interest

There is no reason to believe that any officer or employee of IBM has placed himself in a position in which his loyalties might be thought to conflict. It is worthwhile, however, to repeat the fundamental policy of IBM:

Each employee must be free of any investment or association – whether his own or his family's – which might interfere or be thought to interfere with the independent exercise of his judgment in the best interests of IBM.

A conflict of interest, or the appearance of a conflict, may arise under a variety of circumstances. It is not feasible, however, to describe every such situation, or to prepare a detailed catalog of business ethics. This would run the dual risk of unduly restricting the broad application of the basic policy or of extending it to irrelevant matters.

Still, it might be helpful to give examples of a few of the situations which have been publicized through newspaper reports and legal actions and which clearly are conflicts of interest.

Example: No IBM employee may own, directly or beneficially, any financial interest in any supplier, if in his position the employee influences decisions with respect to IBM's business with that supplier. Clearly included are employees who draw specifications for, recommend, evaluate or approve a supplier's product or service or who participate in the selection of or the arrangement with a supplier.

Example: No employee who in his position influences in any way a decision with respect to IBM's business with a supplier should hold any position with such supplier, whether as a director, officer, employee or agent.

Example: No IBM employee should have an investment of a size which is significant to him in one of our major competitors.

Example: No employee should place himself under an actual or apparent obligation to anyone by accepting gifts or other personal favors which one might believe, or even suspect, were given for the purpose of influencing his business judgment. The acceptance of conventional business courtesies, such as an occasional luncheon would naturally not influence an

employee to disregard the best interests of his employer.
On the other hand, extended entertainment, expensive gifts
or other unusual favors raise justifiable suspicions that they are
given to create an obligation inconsistent with an employee's
responsibility to IBM.

In any case where it is wrong for the employee to do any
of the above things, it is equally wrong for a member of the
employee's immediate family to do so.

Ethical Conduct

Beyond clear cases of conflict of interest, there are situations
which are inconsistent with accepted high standards of business ethics. For instance, an investment by an employee in
a supplier might be improper even though in his position he
does not influence IBM's business decisions with that supplier.
The propriety of such investments must be determined on the
basis of many factors including the IBM position held by the
employee, the amount of the investment and its significance to
the employee, the size of the supplier, and the amount of IBM
business with the supplier. The fundamental principle to keep
in mind is that there cannot be any compromise with high
standards of business ethics. If there is room for suspicion that
an employee's interest or connection with another venture
might affect that employee's judgment in acting for IBM, he
must dispose of that interest or sever that connection.

It is also possible that associations with other business firms,
through directorships, advisory board memberships, or other
affiliation, may give rise to questions of business ethics. An
example is the association of an employee with a firm dealing
primarily in investments, such as a mutual fund. While it is
clear that no employee should be an officer of a mutual fund,
the question of the propriety of an employee serving as a
director depends upon the circumstances. For instance, there
is a difference between a small fund specializing in electronic
stocks and a large, well-established fund with widely diversified

investments and a board of directors composed of well-known industrial and financial executives. The essential test is to consider the reaction of the public to the association of either the employee or the name of the IBM company with the outside venture. If possible embarrassment in the eyes of the public might result, the association should be avoided.

There is another IBM policy involving a different aspect of ethical conduct. This concerns the use or disclosure of inside information, that is to say, information which an IBM employee obtains in the course of his employment. The use or disclosure, intentional or inadvertent, of inside information discredits both the employee and IBM in the eyes of the public, whether that information is used for the financial gain of the employee or to enable others to make such gains. For example, if an employee learns that IBM is about to make or substantially increase a contract with a particular company, it is wrong for that employee to employ that inside information as a basis for making an investment, even if the employee has other reasons for so investing. It is equally wrong for the employee to disclose that information to anyone else for such person's personal gain.

Thomas J. Watson Jr.

Number 6-61: August 9, 1961

IBMers have always been very conscious of their community responsibilities, and have taken an active role in helping to improve the standards of education in our local communities.

American education faces a greater challenge today than ever before. This challenge boils down to simply this: How can we improve our system of education so it can give our children an education adequate to the needs of tomorrow's world?

As a company, we support education financially and provide a number of programs designed to assist school systems. But because American education receives direction at the local level, its really crucial support is what individuals contribute in time, effort, and talent in their own communities.

Managers, especially, have qualifications of leadership and experience that could make them extremely valuable to a local school system. Our schools need many different kinds of assistance, including speakers, seminar leaders, advisors to counselors, specialized instructors and assistants to the school boards, to name but a few.

Certainly all our people should be encouraged to give their support to their local school systems. Under our policy, the company will do everything reasonable to accommodate any employee who needs time off for these activities.

Our education systems need the support and participation of the best minds and talents in the country. Because I believe IBM has a large share of these minds and talents, I think it is appropriate that IBMers try to make an even greater contribution to meeting the educational needs of their communities.

Thomas J. Watson Jr.

Number 7-61: October 6, 1961

Most of my letters to you are stimulated by incidents that come to my attention and seem to me to involve principles more important for the IBM company than the incidents themselves. This letter is no exception. The incident itself is serious, but the principles involved here concern our whole posture as a corporation.

Recently, one of our customers developed a data processing technique and made it available to us as an application of our equipment. This meant, of course, that we could use this application as a selling point. However, some of our people became so enthusiastic about this technique that they neglected to point out to our prospects that it was not ours. In effect, our people encouraged the assumption that it was an IBM technique.

Obviously, our action in this instance was unethical, to say the least. I am telling you about it to make the point that IBM is too fine a company and we have too good a reputation to take false credit for anything.

We have always stood on the record of our actual accomplishments and we must continue to do so. I would be gravely disappointed to hear about any IBMer, whatever his position, who felt that the truth about IBM was not enough of a competitive advantage. In the long run, the only reputation that will endure is the one which is built on what we are, as a company and as individuals, and not on what we may claim to be.

In all of our business dealings, we must be too "big" to be "small" about anything.

Thomas J. Watson Jr.

Number 8-61: December 15, 1961

Each of you, as a manager, should have a clear understanding of IBM's employment procedures. One of them that we want to tell you about here requires especially sensitive handling: hiring employees of our competitors.

As our operations expand, so does our need for more people, many with highly specialized skills and knowledge. We are glad to see all applicants for all kinds of positions, and give equal consideration to everyone who comes to us.

By the same token, we want to be completely straightforward in dealing with applicants employed by other organizations. Managers should avoid any practice which could be considered unfair. There are no clear-cut rules to fit all circumstances. But here are some general guides:

– We should not seek out or contact individuals employed by our competitors (that is, companies which compete with us in a product or service), either ourselves or through a third party, such as an employment agency.

– If an individual, without solicitation, indicates interest in IBM, or answers an advertisement, or approaches us through a third party, we should give him the same consideration we give to all other applicants.

– We should not offer any unusual inducements regarding salary, title, scope of responsibilities, etc.

– We should consider the impact on a competitor's operation that might result from our hiring an employee of that competitor. The department or individual responsible for employment at your location has additional information and should be consulted prior to extending an offer.

– When we make an offer, we should urge that ample notice be given to assure completion of current assignments prior to leaving the competitor.

– If we hire an employee of a competitor, we should instruct him not to disclose to IBM, or use, in performing his job, any confidential information obtained while employed by the competitor.

This is certainly not a complete list. You need to use your own good judgment, discretion and sensitivity in each case. The personnel planning representatives in the field and the personnel managers in the plants, laboratories and division headquarters are prepared at any time to give you advice and guidance.

Object Lesson: The Art of Balanced Sensitivity

This business of being sensitive is probably the toughest part of your job as a manager. Many of the mistakes by managers in the object lessons we have published could be classified as errors in sensitivity. A manager was either insensitive to the needs of his employees or ignored the needs of the company. When a manager is aware of both these needs, he shows balanced sensitivity. Here's a case where just that happened, an object lesson with a hero:

A manager, who had just been promoted into a new job, found that one of his employees – with IBM only four months – was not doing satisfactory work. The former manager was convinced the man was unqualified, but had been reluctant to release him. The reason, as the former manager explained it, was that the man had about five years of experience doing the same kind of work before coming to IBM.

The new manager realized that the longer the problem dragged on, the tougher it would be to solve. Despite the record, he decided to make up his own mind about the employee – as fast as he could get the answers – and do whatever was needed. If the man had ability, the manager wanted to help him turn out a job that would reflect it. If the employee could not perform, in fairness to the company, he would have to be released.

So, the manager took these steps:

- He discussed the situation frankly with the employee. Probing, he learned that the man's experience was not exactly what the former manager had thought. On his employment application, the man had given a true – but general – picture of his work history. The former manager, in a hasty interview, had not gone into enough detail about the man's prior job.
- He gave the employee a special assignment in line with his actual experience. But here, too, the employee's performance was poor.
- He reviewed the case with his own boss and with the personnel people. Then he gave the employee a lower-level assignment, warning him that failure to do a good job would mean separation. Once again, the employee's performance was poor.
- Only after doing everything he could to help the man improve, after seeing that the man knew at all times where he stood, and after giving him ample opportunity to upgrade his work, the manager released the employee.

This manager came to grips with his problem. He acted in fairness to both the employee and IBM. With balanced sensitivity, he settled the case.

Thomas J. Watson Jr.

Number 1-62: January 19, 1962

What attracts the top professionals and specialists? Chances are, it's not what attracts other job applicants. All over the company today, we're interviewing and hiring top professionals with specialized knowledge we need. Occasionally, some of them slip through our fingers. One of the reasons is probably that many of us are using the right "sell," but on the wrong customer.

Traditionally, we've attracted people on the basis of our outstanding business success, our opportunities for advancement in management, and our benefits and job security. These are good, sound inducements and are based on the facts, but they don't attract everyone to the same degree. The highly qualified professional, the specialist we're talking about, often already knows a good deal about our company. If not, he is still probably interested in something else first.

What this person is likely to be looking for is an environment in which he can pursue his professional goals to the maximum of his ability, and achieve real professional recognition, both inside the company, and in his field. Other considerations are usually secondary.

So when we interview a top professional, let's try to present IBM in terms of his interests, his long-term goals. Most important, let's try to show him that IBM is the kind of company – diverse enough and flexible enough – that can match his goals with real opportunities and genuine recognition for achieving them.

Thomas J. Watson Jr.

Number 2-62: June 14, 1962

Recently in a series of lectures at Columbia University I had
the opportunity to talk about the three basic beliefs which I
feel largely account for IBM's success: respect for the individual, giving the very best possible service, and the pursuit
of perfection.

This last proposition – that we cannot settle for anything
less than a superior effort in everything we do – is what I want
to discuss with you here.

The pursuit of perfection means not just enthusiasm for
doing a top-notch job in important things, it means attention
to detail and an itch to innovate and improve in whatever we
have to do. It means to be dissatisfied with the status quo.

This business of ours is built on the need for our society
to deal with details and constantly to find more efficient ways
of dealing with those details. That we, of all people, should
epitomize these skills in our own operations seems self-evident.

I am convinced that our "perfectionism" is one of the main
things that put us out in front – and keeps us out in front.

Now, of course, there are limits to perfectionism. We can
get so bogged down in details that we miss the whole point of
what we are trying to get done. What I am urging is that we
all apply a healthy skepticism, a creative dissatisfaction, at all
times, to whatever we are given to do.

We should never tolerate meaningless tasks, or taboos, or
an inefficient method simply because it's always been done that
way, or because we've been told it's the "IBM way." The "IBM
way," as far as I'm concerned, is whatever way is most efficient,
no matter how it was done in the past.

We ought always to know precisely why a given job is done
in a particular way, and why it is done at all, and why it can't be
done more efficiently, if it must be done at all.

This is the attitude that built our modern industrial society.
It is the attitude that built IBM. I hope we never lose it.

Thomas J. Watson Jr.

Number 3-62: June 26, 1962

Although our size has made it necessary for us to decentralize, to break our operations down into manageable units, we must still operate as the IBM company, as one company.

We are a business with a single mission: to help people solve their problems through the application of data processing and other information handling equipment. There is a close relationship between all parts of our product line. Any major decision in one part of the business inevitably affects many other parts of the business. We are not a group of unrelated businesses tied together by a corporate structure. We are one business.

And this means that every manager in IBM must not only manage his own particular part of IBM, he must manage it as a part of IBM. He must be alert to the needs of the whole company in every decision he makes.

I am somewhat concerned about a tendency I detect in some quarters to operate in isolation, to prefer isolation, to be rather unconcerned about what goes on in the rest of IBM, to assume that all IBM facilities that are out of sight belong to another world. Such provincialism can undermine our corporate strength as quickly as anything I know of.

I hope that each of you will make it his business to know – at least in some general way – what the rest of IBM is doing, so that you can make decisions, not just in the light of conditions in your own area, but with a proper regard for the whole company.

Managers who can do this, who can combine the proprietary concern of a small company manager with breadth of vision, are the kind of managers we need in IBM, and will need increasingly in the future.

Object Lesson: The Best Laid Plans

There's no certainty when a man comes to work that he's going to do a good job. He may reveal – only after he's on board – that he lacks the full quota of talent and interest that the assignment requires. Usually we're right in our evaluation of applicants. But mistakes sometimes happen, and correcting a mistake can sometimes mean separation.

When people leave the business, at their own wish or the company's, they should do so under the best possible circumstances. Unpleasantness and embarrassment don't necessarily go hand-in-hand with separation. Separation can come in an atmosphere of good will. Here's a case in point:

A seemingly well-qualified young man was hired as a programmer trainee. Within weeks, he realized that he was falling far behind his classmates. It was not a matter of intelligence or aptitude, but of interest and concentration. One of his instructors, on his own time, tutored him in the evenings. The instructor thought if he could transmit some of his own enthusiasm for programming, the man would begin to move ahead. But it didn't work. The trainee tried hard, but showed no real improvement.

The trainee, his instructors, and his manager reviewed the problem. They all agreed that he would probably fail the course. He decided to resign.

In a letter to the company, written a few days after he left, he expressed his gratitude for the courtesy that he'd been shown in spite of the fact that he'd been an employee for only a short time. He was impressed too by the manner in which the administrative personnel handled his resignation, but he was most impressed, he said, by the "exceptional efforts" of his instructor, who gave up leisure time to tutor him.

We can't expect all former employees to take the same view. But when an individual leaves the company – regardless of circumstances – we should certainly be sure that we have done everything we could to see that he goes without bitterness and recrimination.

Communication by Whisper

Once a rumor is on the move, what can you do about it? What do you do if a rumor comes to your attention? What if an employee confronts you with a rumor? Should you confirm or deny it?

If you don't know anything about the rumored subject, say so, and say also that you will try to track it down and report back. Then do just that, making sure that your manager hears about the rumor in question.

If you ascertain that the rumor has no foundation in fact, tell the man. If it has some truth to it, and you can confirm it, do so. If it has some truth to it, and you aren't at liberty to discuss it, tell the man simply that. It might not be the answer he wants but it's an answer. And you might ask him not to discuss it either.

All of us in management are committed to, and expected to, keep everyone in the company informed – promptly and thoroughly. Rumors can distort our best intentions and create unending confusion. We can't stop them all. We shouldn't expect to. But we can stop them from getting completely out of hand if we act promptly to confirm, to deny, or to report that we are not at liberty to do either.

Thomas J. Watson Jr.

Number 4-62: August 23, 1962

"I've learned a lot from this appraisal and counseling session. But there's one thing I still don't know. When am I going to get a raise?"

At appraisal and counseling sessions this question – or one like it – is sometimes asked by employees. In handling it properly, you have to keep in mind that, generally, it's not a good idea to mix the subject of pay with appraisal and counseling. Here's why:

- The purpose of your appraisal-counseling session is to review in detail the employee's past performance and help chart future objectives. His attention should be concentrated on that. There should be no wondering, "Will I or won't I get a raise?" If you hand out an increase during the interview, the employee may remember it much more clearly than your specific suggestions for improving his performance.
- Employees shouldn't get the idea that increases come with regularity. Raises should be given as earned, not predetermined by the appraisal and counseling schedule.

Still, if you get a question about money during an appraisal and counseling session, don't try to duck it. Tell the man just where he stands. If he doesn't merit an increase, you should let him know how he can improve his performance to earn one or broaden himself so he can be promoted. If the question comes from someone you plan to give a raise soon, you might point out to him that he could get one before long, if he continues his top-notch performance.

If you think your people have any questions about the relationship of raises to appraisal and counseling sessions, you might review the aims of the program at your next departmental meeting.

Object Lesson: Should You Hire Him?

In hiring an applicant be sure that you first look into all the facts. Of the many people who come to us for jobs, only a few are deliberately concealing information. So you don't want to be overly suspicious or ask irrelevant questions. On the other hand, you can't assume, because someone is poised and personable, he is necessarily able and trustworthy. As you interview an applicant, using the leads provided by the application form, you may suspect he's being evasive. If so, dig deeper into his background. In any case, it's always a good idea to check with his previous employers.

Here's what happened when one of our managers made the mistake of taking what a job applicant said at face value.

This manager interviewed a young man who seemed experienced, alert, intelligent. The applicant had a good personality and a pleasant manner. But his employment record revealed that within the past few years, he'd held a number of different jobs in different sections of the country. There were unexplained time gaps and his salary pattern was uneven.

The manager questioned the applicant about his record. But, since the manager was already sold on the man, he readily accepted his explanations and hired him.

A few months later, the manager learned that his new employee was financially irresponsible – and had been for a long time. There was a string of debts trailing him across the country. At IBM too he had begun to run up large debts to other employees and local merchants. When all this came to light, the employee, as he had done in the past, quit his job and quickly moved away.

The manager could have avoided this whole situation if he had checked thoroughly on the applicant's background and contacted the man's previous employers. Then the manager could have based his decision on facts – not appearances.

Thomas J. Watson Jr.

Number 5-62: September 12, 1962

From time to time, I hear of managers who are somehow too busy to take their vacations. Some of you may feel that this is a commendable attitude. I don't.

If any of us are so busy that we think the company can't get along without us for a while, we're either not properly organized, or we're making ourselves more indispensable than anyone should be. No matter how busy I am, I always manage to take a vacation. Further, I believe if I did not take a vacation, it would not be in the best interests of the IBM company.

Obviously, when you're away your superiors may find it more difficult to get quick answers and your own people will feel your absence in other ways. However, this is no reason not to take your vacation. Also, you should be sure that your people take theirs.

We have a good vacation plan, and for a very good reason. Everybody needs a certain amount of change and rest to stay healthy and to do his job properly. I think you owe it to yourself, as well as to the company, to make sure you take a vacation every year.

Thomas J. Watson Jr.

Number 6-62: October 30, 1962

Recently a trade publication, reporting on an important scientific meeting, mentioned that an IBM speaker substituted for another IBM man who originally had been scheduled to address the group. Although this substitution was made in an orderly and agreeable manner, and well in advance of the engagement, it raised in my mind the whole question of honoring our speaking commitments.

An invitation to address a group gives us a wonderful opportunity to show that group the kind of company we are. And I think you will agree with me that sending a substitute might easily give the impression we don't consider that particular group very important.

It's essential that, when we agree to speak to a group, we do everything we can to keep our word. I certainly hope that no one is using the pressure of business as an easy excuse for backing out of an engagement.

If you should ever have a valid reason – and I would say there aren't very many – for canceling an appointment to speak, I trust you will do everything necessary to avoid inconveniencing the people involved, and of course give plenty of notice and arrange for a qualified replacement.

Honoring our speaking commitments goes a long way toward helping us keep IBM's reputation for dependability. I am convinced that this reputation is so important that we should never miss any opportunity to strengthen it.

Thomas J. Watson Jr.

Number 7-62: November 12, 1962

In a letter to you last year, I spoke of the importance of our personal and collective behavior in building and keeping the good will of the public. I said it was my feeling that the real character of our company shows itself in the way we deal with people on a day-to-day basis.

One of these everyday responsibilities is the way in which we conduct business with thousands of vendors, big and small. The good will of each of them, regardless of size, is important to us.

As most of you know, the purchasing organization at each location is responsible for buying goods and services required by IBM. This responsibility includes all vendor relations and means that each manager, before contacting a vendor, should consult his local purchasing people. But, afterwards, there may be occasions when managers, other than purchasing managers, will deal with vendors or will be in some position to affect our vendor relations.

Recently I learned that in one area of our business we were completely mishandling one aspect of our vendor relationships. Some of our people had been in the habit of settling bills with our vendors beyond the customary ten-day discount period, but taking the discount anyway.

This was "corporate bigness" at its worst. As a large company, we were taking advantage of our vendors. This disturbed me a great deal, because I felt it was grossly unfair. Not only was it wrong at that location, in those circumstances, but also it was an action unworthy of anyone in the entire IBM company.

I believe that in all our dealings with vendors we should be guided by a basic principle: We want always to treat them the same way that we would want to be treated. We have no excuse for ever doing otherwise.

Thomas J. Watson Jr.

Number 1-63: January 31, 1963

"Can a company, no matter how big it is, no matter how impressed it may become with its own importance, ever forget the small courtesies and customary amenities?"

An angry customer wrote and asked us that question recently. And – as I found out – he had cause to be angry. He had purchased one of our products, tried it out and found it was not suitable for his needs. We took it back. But, although we planned to return his money, he had to write to us six times before he got it. We had no intention of evading our commitment to this man. It seemed we were just too busy to answer any of his letters.

I have written to you before about "corporate bigness" and about throwing our weight around in our dealings with small customers and small competitors. My concern over this problem has not diminished. The case I just cited was only one of a number like it that came to my attention in recent months. In each of these cases, we somehow managed to get the customer mad at us, even though we were sometimes in the right – technically.

I am quite aware that we cannot keep everyone happy all the time – but it is extremely important that we try. We are a large company now, and so vulnerable to criticism that we can no longer be satisfied just to be technically correct in our dealings with people. We must be more than that. Our size and our success oblige us to do everything in our power to see that customers, competitors and the public never even think we are unfair, insensitive or impersonal in our dealings with them.

One of the reasons we are successful today is that over the years we have been a good company with which to do business. We have given people what they paid for – and then some. We have been willing to go to almost any length to keep a customer happy. We have always realized that good will is revenue.

We need that spirit today more than ever before. I hope every IBM manager understands this, and makes sure his people understand it too.

Thomas J. Watson Jr.

"Personal" Means Just That

Let's say you're sending a memo to another manager about an unannounced product. To make sure the correspondence isn't read by unauthorized persons, how would you mark the envelope?

You should use: "IBM Confidential."

This would tell the manager's secretary she could open it, add appropriate background material, and give the whole package to her boss.

But when you want only the addressee to see your memo, you should mark the envelope "Personal." However, if the addressee is absent, a reply will be held up until he returns.

As recipient of an "IBM Confidential" memo that came under a "Personal" cover, you should be the judge of how your reply should be marked and sent.

Correspondence is often needlessly marked "Personal" or "IBM Confidential." This only complicates things and weakens security awareness. Just mark to protect information that's really confidential.

On Transfers: Some Do's and Don't's

When an employee asks for a transfer to another location or department, don't ignore it. Even if his request comes when you've got a lot of other things pressing, give it your full attention.

Remember, it may be the most important thing on his immediate horizon.

Talk to him carefully. Find out why he wants the transfer. Maybe he has a family or health problem, or perhaps he wants a change in his assignment or location. If you decide not to approve his request, let him know it – and why – as soon as possible.

Obviously, the final decision on your employee's request will be made by the area to which it's forwarded. You can help cut down delays in reaching that decision by making sure the area has all the information it needs. Keep the employee posted on where things stand, and follow up on his request regularly. And, as soon as you get the final word, pass it on to him. Even if it's unfavorable, he'll know you tried.

Object Lesson: Endorsements

An employee, new to the area, asked his manager to help him find a lawyer. The manager suggested his own attorney. Months later, the employee insisted that, through the lawyer's negligence, the employee's legal affairs had been mishandled. Since the manager had furnished the lawyer's name, and – in the employee's view – vouched for his services, the employee felt that IBM was also vouching for his services.

The manager's mistake was not that he helped his employee, but that he let the employee think he was officially recommending the lawyer. Although the manager didn't say this, he didn't specifically point out it wasn't so.

We want to help an employee with a personal problem whenever we can. But we should never give the impression that the help we offer obligates the company in any way to guarantee it. So, keep these points in mind:

– Don't be insistent about your advice. The employee shouldn't feel that he'll be in an embarrassing spot if he doesn't follow it.
– If you don't feel qualified to give names of professionals, don't. Your guesswork won't help an employee.
– Give several names if you have some reasonable basis for doing so. If there's an IBM doctor or lawyer at your location, you could ask him for help in finding qualified persons. The Personnel people would also be in a position to lend a hand.
– If the employee asks for your own preference, you can give it to him. But make it crystal clear that this is a personal evaluation.

Thomas J. Watson Jr.

Number 3-63: May 17, 1963

I'm impressed by the attitude with which most of our managers approach their jobs. Occasionally I meet a few who have an attitude which concerns me. These managers give the impression that they seldom really question their own operations; they hardly ever ask, "Why?"

Constantly questioning our operations is essential to good management, especially in IBM. I know that we are all busy, but I suggest that each of us should make time, once in a while, to take a look at our areas as a visitor might, and ask why we do certain things in a certain way. This is the kind of searching attitude that results in real innovation. When you ask this kind of question you are bound to come up with something new and better.

Of course we want all of our people to have this attitude, not just the managers. The way to encourage this feeling is for all of us in management to be open to questions at all times. And we should impress upon our people that IBM needs their ideas, whether big or small, just as long as their ideas help us to move ahead. You know best just how to stimulate this inquiring attitude. It was this kind of attitude that helped IBM to progress in the past and will help IBM to continue to progress in the future.

In the months and years ahead, problems will come faster and faster and we will have less and less time to solve them. What we need more than anything is to see problems before they emerge fully grown. I would say that the best way to do this is to ask, "Why?"

Thomas J. Watson Jr.

Number 4-63: July 23, 1963

Object Lesson: Unreasonable Instructions

Recently, one of our suppliers wrote a letter to our company.
He was very unhappy with IBM, and understandably so.

For over six years, his company had been performing a
service for IBM at one of our locations. His service, according
to our local people, had always been satisfactory. One day
he was abruptly told that our future business would be placed
with another organization. The only reason given him by
our local people was: "The change was ordered by Corporate
Headquarters." The background on this situation was:

– This location, like a number of others in IBM, had been
   using a local company to handle this particular service.
   Corporate Headquarters, after reviewing the requirements
   of all locations, had found that IBM could save a substantial
   amount if this service were obtained from a few suppliers
   at centralized spots.
– The change meant that some locations had to terminate
   the services of their local suppliers and utilize other firms
   located at the consolidated points.
– When the decision was made to put this new program into
   effect, the only instructions given to the locations involved
   were to discontinue using their old local suppliers and to
   place all future business with the prescribed new ones.
   No reasons were given for making the change.

It is easy to see why this supplier, who had served us well for
years, was most unhappy when he was told only that he would
get no more business from us because a change was ordered
by Corporate Headquarters. We can learn two management
lessons from this experience:

– Whenever you ask someone to carry out a decision, tell
   him the "why" of it, not just to do it.
– If you are ever asked to carry out something affecting
   outsiders or employees which makes no sense to you, be

sure to find out the "why" of it so you can understand and explain it intelligently.

How to Handle a Reference?

Do you know what to do when you're asked for a reference about an employee or former employee?

Although some managers may not realize it, IBM has a clear-cut policy for handling references and other kinds of personnel inquiries. It's designed to protect the privacy of employees and to cooperate with other organizations which have a legitimate interest in them. To be sure a reference request is handled properly, here's what you should do:

– Whether the request comes to you by mail or phone, regardless of who contacts you, pass it on to the people in your location responsible for personnel matters. They'll release only certain details about an individual's employment history, such as the period he was employed, his position and department. Salary isn't mentioned unless the employee permits it.

– If you're asked for a personal reference, of course you may give one. If the request is made by phone, we suggest you call back, to be certain of the inquirer's identity. If your answer is in writing, to either a written or phone request, don't use IBM stationery. In any case, you should point out that it's a personal, not a company, statement.

Thomas J. Watson Jr.

Number 5-63: September 23, 1963

A number of cases involving IBM suppliers have focused attention on the importance of good supplier relations. We do business with tens of thousands of firms, large and small, and it is important that we always conduct our affairs with them in a highly ethical and businesslike way.

These cases did not suggest that our basic purchasing policies and practices needed overhauling. They suggested that all of us in IBM – and not just the Purchasing people – need to be more sensitive to the problems and expectations of the supplier doing business with IBM.

We need the good will of these suppliers, just as we need the good will of customers and stockholders and the public in general. The attached booklet* was prepared to guide you in this area. We suggest you discuss it with your people, where appropriate, and that you keep it for reference.

*Current booklet available from Mechanicsburg (order number G508-0001).

Thomas J. Watson Jr.

Number 6-63: October 2, 1963

I am becoming more and more concerned with the "creeping paralysis" in decision-making in IBM. We're not as fast on our feet as we should be. We often respond too slowly to the challenges and opportunities of our growing industry.

The reason for this is not that we don't have a fine corps of managers. I think we have the best in the world. The reason is that too many managers are not using all the authority that has been delegated to them.

There seems to be entirely too much double checking, too much "group-think," too many committee decisions, too many levels of approval before a proposal can be translated into action. I suspect there is probably as much "selling" effort inside IBM, among ourselves, as there is out in the field with customers.

We need to push more decision-making down to the level where the decisions are carried out. This means delegation, and delegation means delegating a chance to fail, as well as a chance to succeed. Failure can develop good managers just as well as success can.

From now on, I would like each of you to make as many decisions as you can on your own and reduce to the lowest possible level the amount of consultation, concurrence and approval involved.

I am not asking you to throw all caution to the winds and end up as dead heroes. But I am asking you to think more about getting the job done quickly, and with a minimum of "playing it safe." Every time you think about getting approval or concurrence, instead, ask yourself, "Can I make this decision here and now, on my own?"

We are moving in fast company these days, and we simply have to move faster than anyone else if we want to lead the race.

Thomas J. Watson Jr.

Number 1-64: January 31, 1964

Every manager wants to run a tight ship, but few of us want to be a Captain Bligh. Too much strictness is bad, but too much permissiveness invites trouble of its own. In management, as in walking a tightrope, balance is everything.

An example is the coffee break. Starting out as a quick morning trip to a vending machine or coffee cart, it can grow into a prolonged social occasion at the start of the day, a repeat performance at eleven or so, and another get-together in mid-afternoon. From a convenience, the coffee break becomes a ritual, and it becomes a painful duty for a manager to curtail it.

Getting time off for personal reasons is another privilege that could be abused. And you're inviting abuse if you treat time off requests automatically. Such requests may well be justified, but you should be satisfied that they are when you grant them. The decision is yours and you should make it each time the question comes up. Don't let habit force that decision.

The point of all this is that if you don't exercise positive control of a situation, you're going to find it awfully tough to get things back to the way you want them. Remember, it's your job to run your department by properly exercising the authority that's been given you. And authority, like muscles, can get flabby through lack of exercise.

Object Lesson: Managing a Change

In our growing company, organizational changes – or individual and group transfers – may be a way of life to many of us. But we still can't forget that not everybody takes changes in stride. Furthermore, if these changes are thrust upon employees without sufficient warning, explanation or consideration, problems are certain to occur.

For example, at one of our locations a new operation was recently brought in which made it necessary to rearrange office space. It meant that some local people would have to move out to provide space for the incoming group. Instead of the local people being prepared for the shift, the new group was simply moved in without warning. Some of the local people were actually dispossessed before new space had been arranged. Needless to say, things didn't go very smoothly.

Any change, even if it makes some people happy, is bound to disappoint others or bring on their disapproval. We can't always help this. But there are some things we can do to make the transition pleasant – or if not pleasant, at least not painful. Whenever you are making a change involving a group, or an individual, remember to:

- Let your people know about it in advance whenever possible. Tell them as early as you can, and as much as you can.
- Explain just what the change is, who and what it will involve, and why.
- Be considerate of the feelings of the people involved. Show your employees by words and actions your genuine concern for their fears and uneasiness.

We want our people to be flexible in accepting change and growth at IBM. They won't be unless we convince them that their feelings are always considered when a change is made.

Thomas J. Watson Jr.

We in IBM have long had a reputation for excellence. This is
certainly reflected in our buildings, our furnishings, our
products, and in our general style of doing things. But I am
becoming more and more concerned that some of us may be
confusing our pattern of excellence with a set of imaginary
standards, and then using these standards as an excuse for
spending money extravagantly.

Of course we want IBM to look good in all things. But
looking good, to my mind, means appropriate, not expensive.
To look and act prosperous can be sound business practice.
But to spend out of proportion to need is foolish and can
make us look ostentatious. When we spend money – on a
product or service – we should not aim to meet a mythical IBM
standard, but rather spend what is needed for that particular
time and place.

It is really a question of utility versus prestige. In most
things, all that we should really be looking for is utility.
In those instances where prestige is a necessary and desirable
part of an expenditure, such as in the case of the design of
our buildings, which stand as an advertisement of us in the
eyes of the general public, the extra cost is certainly justified.
Again, good judgment should dictate that only that amount
of prestige should be paid for which serves a useful purpose
in our business. By all means, let's continue to do things
right. But let's make sure that doing things right also means
getting the job done efficiently and economically.

Thomas J. Watson Jr.

Number 4-64: June 22, 1964

I would like to discuss with you the dangers of what I call hearsay policies or orders.

Recently I learned about a manager who – against his better judgment – was directing his operation down the wrong road because he believed he was following policy established at some previous time higher up in the company. As it turned out, the manager had never personally read this policy; he had only "understood" that it existed.

It seems to me that when we, as managers, do things like this, we violate some principles of sound management.

We should never operate on the basis of hearsay policies or orders. Instead, let's always find out the facts and manage on that basis. The hearsay may be neither true nor timely. Furthermore, even if there is such a policy – or order – and it is not appropriate for the situation at hand, let's challenge it. We must continue to intelligently question present practices to assure that the IBM company operates on an effective, up-to-date basis.

Traditions, "understandings" and ancient practices are seldom good guides to management in a growing company. More than ever before, IBM needs managers who are not afraid to challenge precedent, who accept nothing on hearsay, and are not afraid to take a stand and criticize antiquated or improper rules.

Thomas J. Watson Jr.

Number 5-64: July 10, 1964

There still seems to be some misunderstanding on the subject of telephone courtesy. So, it may be well to discuss it again, even though we have mentioned it before in *Management Briefing*.

The proper and courteous use of the telephone seems an elementary thing. However, again and again, I hear of cases in which managers – either because they don't know or don't care – seem to completely overlook the fact that courtesy in using the telephone is as necessary as courtesy in any other part of our business life.

We spend so much of our time each day on the telephone, and so large a part of our business is conducted this way, I believe we should all make an attempt to make our telephone dealings work for – instead of against – us.

I have attached to this letter some guidelines which may help you in this area.

Telephone Courtesy: Some Guidelines

- Whenever possible, a manager should answer his own phone. Of course, there are some times when it is impractical to do this. For example, it is not a good practice to take phone calls during a meeting with outsiders or IBMers. It's better to arrange for someone to inform callers that you are in a meeting and ask if you can return the call later. You should also make similar arrangements when you are having a personal discussion – such as an appraisal and counseling session – with an employee. The important thing about answering your own phone is that, even though you may not be able to do so all the time, you still set an excellent example for others by trying your best to be personally responsive, whenever possible, to your calls.
- When making or receiving a call, don't assume that the other party will recognize your voice. Identify yourself immediately.

– When a secretary answers your phone, she should not ask for a caller's name before stating whether you are in. This might easily give the impression she is screening your calls – that you are "in" to some people, but not to others.

– Secretaries and operators can often improve your efficiency by helping you place calls – provided this is done in a polite way which won't offend the other party. If a call is placed for you, make sure that you are the first person your party speaks to and that he is never kept waiting for you. One way to do this is to have your secretary call your party's secretary and, after reaching her, put you on the phone to ask for him. In any event, be certain to be on the line when he picks up. Since you are initiating the call, it's very discourteous to ask the other party to assume the inconvenience of waiting for you to come on the phone.

– If you are using a speaker box, it's only common courtesy to mention it to the other party and state the name of anyone else present in your office.

– When you receive an outside call and you're not the person to handle the matter, remember you are representing IBM. Make it your business to see that the caller gets the information he wants, or is put in touch directly with the right person without any further referrals.

Thomas J. Watson Jr.

There have been several occasions recently when IBM managers have indicated a lack of understanding of their basic responsibilities in the area of managing people. As a large company, we find it necessary to have staff specialists who are skilled in a particular area and who can be very helpful in giving us specialized advice and counsel. However, no manager should ever feel he can delegate his basic duties – or decisions – to these staff people.

The job of managing people involves five basic duties. They are: to employ; to teach; to supervise; to promote people who deserve it; and to discharge, when that is necessary. My father always emphasized the importance of these duties and he used to add that "If you give enough thought and attention to the employment, to the education, and to the supervision of men you will have very little discharging to do."

We've grown a lot bigger as a company since then, but these fundamentals still apply. A manager still manages his department, even though we may have staff specialists to help us. And although you review decisions – such as the separation of an employee – with your own manager, it's important to remember that it's you who must make these decisions. If you do, you'll find that managing your people and projects will be a great deal simpler.

I realize that being a manager is tough work. It means you have a heavy load to carry. But it also means you have a lot of authority to help you do the job the way it should be done. I think you should use this authority. Unless you do, you just make the job all the harder. And if you do it, and do it well, the reward and personal satisfaction you will find is very great indeed.

Thomas J. Watson Jr.

Number 7-64: October 15, 1964

Occasionally I hear about an employee getting upset because he thinks IBM is violating his rights in the matter of personal investments. I think it would help to clarify our position on business ethics.

We have no intention of infringing on any employee's right to invest his money in any way he chooses, as long as he doesn't embarrass or adversely affect his relationship with the company by the investment. But being part of IBM does oblige us to avoid two kinds of investments: those which create a conflict of interest, and those based on inside information.

A conflict of interest means an employee is involved in investments or associations – whether his own or his family's – which might interfere or be thought to interfere with the independent exercise of his judgment in the best interests of IBM.

The second restraint is based on the idea of a free market, which assumes that everyone trading on that market has access to the same information. If an IBM employee makes an investment based on information he obtained on the job, he is taking unfair advantage of investors who do not have that knowledge. He is also violating the company's confidence by using restricted information – corporate property – for his personal gain.

I feel it's important that you understand and live by these principles – and that you do your best to see that your people also understand and follow them. If there are people who feel the company is being unreasonable, and can't see and accept the rightness of these requirements, it's hard for me to believe they can do an effective job at IBM. As a general rule, I suggest that when you have some doubt in your mind about the propriety of an investment, you should not make it.

Thomas J. Watson Jr.

Number 8-64: November 18, 1964

In the past few months there has been an alarming increase in the number of leaks of confidential IBM information to persons outside the company. This has become especially evident in reports carried in industry trade publications which often are too accurate to be mere idle speculation by editors. In two instances developments still under wraps in the laboratory were described in the trade press. In another case the detailed on-order situation for the System/360 was published.

Regardless of how such confidential information gets out, IBM suffers. When a competitor gets an upper hand on IBM because of some relative weakness in technology, marketing, or service on our part, we accept the lesson, redouble our efforts, and try to win the next round. But we simply cannot afford to take losses because of security breaches. They are irreparable.

There can be several direct effects of leaks on our immediate and long-range plans, and, therefore, upon our relative success. Our competitors can find out where our research effort is concentrated and what products we have in development. Our marketing position can be damaged by the revelation of unannounced product information. There can even be legal complications since the leakage might be interpreted as a deliberate attempt by IBM to discourage competitors from selling their current products.

Following is a more detailed outline of the security problem in IBM and in our industry today. I want to be sure that every manager understands exactly what we are talking about in this regard and passes the message along to his or her people. The damage to the company that accrues when security is loose can be severe. It is everybody's job to guard against this.

The Thin Edge of the Industrial Security Breach

Here are some examples of recent leaks. An IBM manager took a phone call from a reporter, tersely answering the innocent-sounding questions that lay within his area of competence. But the published report didn't look very innocent when it appeared in a data processing newsletter. It discussed in detail what IBM planned to do with certain systems being returned by customers after installation of the System/360 computers, and discussed current and anticipated revenues in detail. Most of the material came from an unidentified source, but the manager's comments were made to appear as confirmation of trade talk.

Another newsletter reported that it had been told by insiders at a specified IBM facility that we were working on a prototype of a machine that would take the company into a new field. The type of machine was also specifically described, as well as estimated costs, delivery dates, marketing potential, and so forth.

An employee spoke of an unannounced product to a friend. A few days later a columnist on a major daily newspaper several hundred miles away called a local IBM office to get confirmation of a story he'd received in the mail about that product – from the employee's friend.

When a thousand IBMers know a secret, it is no longer a secret. Several weeks ago, an industry publication carried an account of key marketing plans and data with such a wealth of detail that it could only have come from an official source. On investigation, it came to light that this highly proprietary information had been disseminated so broadly within IBM that its sensitivity and importance went unrecognized.

In another instance, a decision was made to announce a major product at an industry-wide conference. Before the announcement could be made, however, it was planned to discuss it with a customer who had been closely involved in the development of a prototype of the product. But before the customer was contacted and only one day after the decision to announce was made, a competitor told the same customer of IBM's intentions. The leak had been accurate, amazingly fast – and highly embarrassing to IBM.

As far as is known, all of these leaks were unintentional.

In a flagrant case, however, an IBM employee who had been offered a bribe, intentionally furnished a representative of an outside organization with highly confidential data. Confronted with the evidence, the employee admitted his guilt and was dismissed from IBM.

There are many other indications of how difficult it is to keep IBM secrets secret. But there are several ways we can help.

- We should never discuss highly confidential subjects, such as unannounced products, costs, potential plant sites, transfers of products between divisions, and so forth, except within IBM, and then only on a "need to know" basis.
- We must assume that the press may be represented, personally or otherwise, wherever we go. Let's realize there's no such thing as a closed meeting if non-IBMers are sitting in. You should be prepared to share whatever you say there with a wider audience, including perhaps the readers of an industry publication.
- When in doubt as to whether you can risk having a statement reported, check the people in your division whose job it is to handle this kind of problem and all clearance questions.
- Don't deal with the press yourself, unless there's no choice. It's full of risks. Instead, use the Information people at your location or at divisional headquarters; they're professionals and can be helpful.
- Keep reminding people who work for you that they're to discuss proprietary information only on the job. Employees sign a statement when they're hired promising not to reveal IBM secrets. Doing so is grounds for discharge.

Not everything that happens inside the walls of the company is top secret. But we can't pretend that secrets exist only in spy stories. Wherever there is an IBM technical facility, there will be people around trying to discover what's happening inside. If we're careless, speak too loudly or in the wrong place, we shouldn't be surprised to find interesting reading in a trade paper.

The security problem is not a new one, but here is some background on why it is growing.

Newspapers and, more particularly, trade magazines are active nowadays in all matters relating to data processing. Press coverage of the field has expanded as rapidly as the industry itself. There are about three times as many magazines, newspapers and newsletters specializing in data processing and automation as there were ten years ago. The situation is competitive and reporters use ingenuity and energy to get stories first – before they happen, if possible. Recently, for example, the exact text of an IBM internal announcement was carried in a newsletter less than a week after it was posted on company bulletin boards.

Members of the industry press attend seminars and technical conferences; they keep in touch with scientific people who may have friends in industry; they talk to vendors and customers of industrial organizations; they call employees directly, ostensibly wanting only confirmation of details already known. What often happens is that the employee will unknowingly spill the beans. The published story can be accurate, full, fair – and harmful to IBM.

Thomas J. Watson Jr.

I recently received a letter from a college professor of mathematics that disturbed me. He had written one of our locations for summer employment. Thirty days later, his letter was acknowledged by stating that he would hear shortly from a specific manager at another location. The next reply was not from the IBMer mentioned earlier, but a different individual who referred him to still another plant location for prompt action. To conclude this pathetic story, the last location never did reply. The professor's impressions were obvious – a loss of respect for our company and our people.

In another instance coming to my attention, a customer inquired as to how to contact me for a speaking engagement. The request dutifully and unimaginatively followed the chain of divisional command, and thirty days later the customer was told to write me a personal letter of invitation.

Attitudes and procedures that reap results such as the above create impressions of the worst kind and do far greater harm in fostering an attitude completely inconsistent with that for which all of us are striving.

While we have discussed the matter of responsible and responsive handling of communications in previous *Management Briefings*, let me again emphasize the basic elements.

–   The recipient of any communication has a responsibility as part of his job to respond quickly and effectively to the matter (normally 48 hours). If a referral is necessary, he should make certain it is the proper referral and subsequent buck-passing will not be necessary. If the matter needs lengthy investigation, a prompt acknowledgment should be made.
–   If the volume of correspondence makes individual control impossible, management should make certain that proper control procedures are in force to insure that all correspondence is completed and on time.

I am relying on each of you as a manager to insure that the proper attitude and procedures in this sensitive area are maintained. In the final analysis, the impressions of the general public toward IBM are indelibly made by the style in which we communicate.

Thomas J. Watson Jr.

Number 2-65: March 26, 1965

In the past few months, two appeals to my office have been made by employees who were released from IBM for violating our policy prohibiting employees from accepting gifts from suppliers. One of these individuals was reinstated in the company; the other was not.

The man who was not reinstated had been a member of a purchasing department. Here our policy was clearly and crisply stated. The man was fully aware of our policy and realized that he had committed a violation of it.

The man whose dismissal was not upheld was a member of another department. This department, while equally sensitive from the standpoint of relations with vendors, did not have in the hands of its employees a clear and crisp statement of our policy. The statement was so imprecisely worded that it could result in an honest misinterpretation. This man's manager had not verbally emphasized and explained the policy and its intent to the man and his fellow employees. Since, under these circumstances, there could have been an honest misinterpretation of policy, his release was reversed.

It would be unfair to discharge an employee for failure to comply with a policy which the company had stated so poorly and imprecisely that honest men could interpret it in different ways. The former, imprecise language was immediately withdrawn in this department and the precise language used in the purchasing department was substituted for it. From that point on, any violation of this policy in this department would be treated in the same manner as it was in the purchasing department.

It is emphasized that what is involved here is not condoning a breach of policy, but a recognition on the part of the company that it would be unfair to discharge a person for not following a policy when the company had itself failed to state the policy in clear, understandable terms that were not subject to honest misinterpretation.

Although this individual was reinstated for the reason just stated, let there be no mistaking the meaning of the rule. All gifts are unacceptable, whether they're worth five dollars or a thousand. Except for an occasional and routine business lunch, no entertainment or special treatment should be accepted either. An employee who is offered a gift or entertainment should report the fact to his manager immediately.

One of our strongest assets is a reputation for honesty and square dealing, and we cannot afford to give an impression that we favor one person or company above another for any reason other than merit. The acceptance of any gift can be interpreted as creating an obligation which may not be in IBM's best interests.

Because many IBMers at one time or another will have to work with individuals outside the company, I hold every manager personally responsible for insuring that all of his people know our position on this subject.

Thomas J. Watson Jr.

Number 3-65: April 7, 1965

A few weeks ago, several Speak Up!s were received which questioned the application of the policy on liquor to purely social functions arranged by IBM Clubs. As a result of these Speak Up!s, the current policy was reviewed, and without changing the fundamental principles, I feel that the following new interpretation is in order. This would make it clear that our policy on liquor, as I have stated before, is not meant to influence any employee's life outside the business. The first two principles of the liquor policy are:

– Liquor is not served on company premises.
– Liquor is not a part of IBM business meetings; that is, those held by the company itself to conduct its own internal affairs.

These two principles will be retained as stated and require no further interpretation.

– The third principle is that liquor is not served at official company social affairs, such as family dinners, children's Christmas parties, Watson trophy dinners at plant locations, IBM Club installation dinners, recognition dinners for the Systems Engineering Symposium, the Hundred Percent Club and Corporate Awards, company picnics and Quarter Century Club events.

Purely social IBM Club activities, when they are held off company premises and paid for on a personal basis, are not included under this principle.

Thomas J. Watson Jr.

Number 4-65: June 2, 1965

It's become clear from information reaching me that some managers don't understand the purpose of the Tuition Refund Plan and what their responsibilities are in relation to it.

Here's an example. At one of our plants, a production machine operator asked for his manager's approval to enroll under the Tuition Refund Plan in courses leading to a degree in accounting. But the manager said, "Since you're a machine operator and the courses have nothing to do with your job, they wouldn't be eligible. Even if I approve them, my manager would probably turn them down."

The Plan is there to encourage personal development of employees, to help them do their current jobs more effectively and to increase their potential for performing more challenging jobs in the future.

But this manager had far too narrow an interpretation of the Plan's aims. He ignored the employee's potential for development, and overlooked the fact that accounting is very much a part of IBM's operations and needs. He also interpreted his own responsibilities as a manager too narrowly when he spoke of getting his own manager's approval. The immediate manager's approval is all that's required since it's he who has the clearest view of an employee's talents and interests.

When we don't understand the company's programs and don't administer them consistently, we're falling down seriously in doing our jobs as managers.

Thomas J. Watson Jr.

Number 5-65: July 27, 1965

A vital factor in the success of any business is the quality of its management decisions, and this quality is directly related to the facts upon which the decisions are based. Every one of us plays a role in this decision-making process. And while no manager can have a perfect batting average, his average can be vastly improved with timely and accurate facts on which to base his actions.

When you observe a situation or are asked for information, you become a key element in the ultimate action that is taken. Your decision on whether to transmit information and what kind of facts to forward can be the vital ingredient in the success of the final decision. Unfortunately, sometimes in IBM there is a tendency to pass reports up through levels of management based on insufficient facts or facts biased by emotion. What is worse, some reports which should be made are not made at all, simply because the news is bad. The result has been some serious mistakes which could have been avoided.

Here is an example of what can happen when the decision-making process breaks down through misinformation:

When it became apparent that our position with two of our largest scientific customers was seriously jeopardized, all of the reports came back that the problem was our price. A great deal of management activity, decision, and action was thus based on this information. It was only at the eleventh hour that it was suddenly discovered that in truth the real problem lay in the technological deficiency of our equipment. Thus, when the proper decisions based on the correct facts could finally be made, it was too late and we lost these two valued customers.

We want to keep the IBM company alert, responsive, aggressive, and always a little dissatisfied with our position. We want to place management emphasis where it belongs – on major problems. To do so, management must be informed accurately and responsibly at all times. Every manager must recognize his responsibility to transmit information that is not only timely, but also substantive and objective.

When you are in the position of making a decision or of communicating information upward for others to make a decision, ask yourself these questions:

- Am I satisfied that the information is factual and complete?
- Am I satisfied that it is free of emotional bias?

Unless you can answer these questions positively, you should suspend transmission until better, more accurate, and disciplined data is obtained.

Thomas J. Watson Jr.

Number 6-65: November 2, 1965

Ordinarily we don't argue with success. Sometimes, though, success itself can create problems. A case in point: IBM's System/360. The outstanding market acceptance of this new product has resulted in a severe strain on many of our people.

As an example, for many months a large number of manufacturing employees have been on a continuing, planned overtime basis. Many of them work every Saturday so that both direct and supporting departments can operate together for maximum effectiveness. This kind of schedule is tough, not just physically, but in every sense. It leaves little time for relaxation – it means postponing trips to football games with the children, visits to grandparents out of state, and other personal plans.

Why has this extensive scheduled overtime been necessary? For these reasons:

- Customer demand for System/360 has been so heavy that it would be impossible to meet our delivery deadlines on a normal work schedule.
- System/360 involves us with a totally new technology. This means we're still making engineering changes, still adjusting to new vendor relationships.
- We're facing some very able competitors. Without a stepped-up schedule, we'd risk their catching up.
- We're carrying out an assignment that in many respects is one of the largest and most complex ever given to an industrial electronics organization – almost a complete replacement of our principal product line.

In view of these realities, the company feels justified in asking employees to put in extra time. It feels justified in excusing employees only for medical reasons, or for other reasons that are equally compelling. On the other hand, we realize there are times when an employee will not be able to work on a particular evening or weekend. But if he can't work scheduled overtime on a regular basis, management will attempt to reassign him to an area where overtime isn't needed.

Why don't we hire more people? We are hiring more people – to meet long-range requirements. But if we bring in people to meet our current peak needs, we will have a personnel surplus when the peak is past. And a personnel surplus makes it more difficult to maintain full employment.

The company recognizes the hardships of this working climate and the sacrifices many employees are making each week. Every manager should make it his business to talk to everyone in his department who is on scheduled overtime assignment and explain what's involved for them and for the company.

Thomas J. Watson Jr.

Number 7-65: November 29, 1965

How many managers still think that an employee is "off limits" if he asks questions about his personnel folder? Probably a good many do. And the main reason is habit.

For some time now, IBM has recognized an employee's right to ask questions about his own employment record. Generally it's a healthy sign, and we should encourage him to do it. Sometimes, he's just curious about what's in his personnel folder. In other cases, he's concerned that it may contain an old management remark that could interfere with his career. As a manager, you can help him learn a lot about himself from that folder and dispel his concerns about the contents.

Probably you don't keep personnel folders in your own bailiwick, but the personnel manager, or whoever else has them at your location, can arrange for you to review them. Information about salary and job progress, if it's not already in the folder, can be had from the salary administration or payroll people.

You don't help an employee by evading his questions or by treating him as a trespasser on private property. Talk to him honestly and directly, and as a general rule show him whatever he wants to see. Naturally, there will be exceptions, such as credit reports, medical documentation, or anything else obtained in confidence. You should also reassure him that only recent performance data is kept in his personnel folder unless it is a letter of commendation, or a similar item, which would be kept permanently. Other documents, including appraisal forms, are kept for three years and then destroyed. However, appraisals may be kept for a maximum of five years if the employee has not been interviewed annually.

You should make it your business to review the folders of all your people. Be reasonably familiar with them, whether the employees have questions or not. And reviewing folders is a good way to get to know about the performance, abilities and interests of people when they're transferred into your department or you go into a new area.

When an employee asks a question you can't answer, go back to his folder. Then discuss it with him. If he wants more information than you can give, you should – if he wishes – arrange for him to speak to the people at your location who handle personnel matters.

Thomas J. Watson Jr.

Number 1-66: January 11, 1966

Effective control of routine business expenses has always been a good measure of taut, lean management in a corporation. With the unusual pressures and expenditures facing us in our massive System/360 effort, there is danger of letting this factor slip to a low priority in our management thinking. We must not let this happen. It is more important now than ever before that IBM get full value for every dollar spent.

Evidence that we have considerable room for improvement presents itself in many ways. For example, in the travel expense area, when I hear of employees taking trips without any prior management approval, of meetings being called of all plants when a representative group from nearby plants would serve the purpose, of two or more people going on a trip that one person should handle, then I must conclude that a substantial reduction in this expense category is possible without materially affecting our ability to do business. A reasonable percentage reduction here would result in really significant dollar savings.

Travel is only one of the many expense areas where value judgments must be made daily and on a very widespread basis. You managers are the ones who must apply these judgments and by your active attention reverse any trend toward looseness in attitude. It is only through this day-to-day attention that expense awareness will become and remain second nature in IBM. Only through your efforts can we sensibly make the significant improvements that must be made in these areas. I know I can count on your support in doing so.

Thomas J. Watson Jr.

Number 2-66: July 25, 1966

From time to time it becomes important to refresh our thinking about various tenets of the business. Few of these tenets are so important as our Employee Relations Principles. For your guidance, a statement of these principles follows:

Employee Relations Principles

Basic IBM guides relative to decisions and actions in employee relations are stated in the following principles. They reflect the kind of company IBM is and wants to continue to be. These principles serve as a guide in the man-manager relationships which affect all of us and influence our progress in the business.

The foundation of these principles is a belief in the day-to-day application of the Golden Rule. The statement, "Do unto others as you would have others do unto you," implies a degree of mutual respect and responsibility on the part of the employee as well as on that of the company.

Respect for the Individual

The rights of the individual should always be respected. It is a mark of good management to be sensitive to the needs of employees, and managers should be constantly alert to give proper credit for outstanding performance.

Fairness in Promotions

When employees are being considered for promotion, primary emphasis should be given to performance. Consideration should also be given to the individual's skills, capabilities, experience, and any unique requirement of the job to be filled. Whenever possible, promotions are filled from within the company. Only in exceptional cases, where the properly qualified individual is not available within IBM, do we go outside the company. By conscious application of this principle we can assure fairness in promotions.

Working Conditions

IBM does everything reasonable to provide working conditions that are safe, pleasant and efficient, and to supply the finest working equipment that we can buy or create.

Communications

Each employee has the right to know where he stands at all times and to receive full information on matters directly or indirectly affecting his job. Every employee shall have the opportunity for regular, individual appraisal and counseling sessions with his manager.

It is equally essential that avenues of upward communication from employees to management be kept open and used to channel information to those who can take needed action. IBM welcomes constructive criticism. No employee need fear reprisal or reprimand for questioning a practice or making a constructive suggestion. The value of two-way communications between the employee and the company cannot be over-emphasized.

Opportunities

IBM believes in equal opportunity for every employee or applicant for employment irrespective of race, sex, religion or national origin. IBM is constantly seeking to employ outstanding individuals. As an objective, the company tries to maintain continuous employment for all satisfactory employees.

Continuing personal development is vital to the success of each individual and to the business. IBM will continue to help employees increase their skills and knowledge through training programs and company support of education, both on the job and on the employee's own time.

Compensation

The company intends to provide compensation and total benefits which are equal to or greater than similar benefits provided by other leading companies. It is part of our basic philosophy that pay and recognition are primarily based on performance. An IBM objective is to offer special recognition and the most significant salary increases to those who make outstanding contributions.

Thomas J. Watson Jr.

Number 3-66: September 21, 1966

An important part of every manager's responsibility is to explain company policies and decisions to the people he manages. To announce them is not enough. A good manager must be ready to discuss and explain them.

In recent months, a number of Speak Up! letters have indicated that some managers are not adequately answering important employee questions about company policies. Sometimes, when employees have raised difficult questions, they have been brushed off with such frustrating replies as "it's company policy," or "the decision was made by Corporate" (or by division headquarters or by some other higher authority) – and given no additional information.

One employee who tried unsuccessfully to obtain more information about a recent management decision wrote:

> "The real injustice in this whole case is the double talk.... I do not want to be unreasonable in this matter, but I feel that I deserve an honest answer."

Another wrote:

> "… their answers are evasive and noncommittal and as such unsatisfactory. The answer given was 'Corporate Policy.'"

Double talk and buck-passing are symptoms of weak management. They invariably create confusion and resentment, and the employee will begin to think he is a victim of a system instead of a member of a team.

Every manager at any level should know and understand the reasons for the policies which affect him and his people. If he does not have the facts when questioned, he is expected to turn to his manager and get them.

There may be times, for example, when the issue ranges beyond the business and into the area of public controversy, when a manager feels that as a matter of conscience he cannot permit himself to be morally associated with a company policy or action. In such an event, the manager should give his people the facts, explain the policy or action and, if he chooses, simply say that he disagrees with it.

A manager has one other key responsibility in this area – the responsibility for evaluating regularly the policies and practices affecting his people and his operation. He must make certain that they are always current and appropriate. He should not hesitate to question or propose changes for those which he considers outdated or no longer applicable.

Effective operating practices – properly understood by those who must carry them out – provide the only sound basis for effective business operations.

Thomas J. Watson Jr.

In September and October, *Fortune* magazine published a two-part series of articles aimed at describing how the IBM company brought out System/360. Since these articles were published, I've been asked by many people how I liked them. Because much of these articles dealt with gossip, with the opinions of a few people, and because they overplayed internal dissension and chaos, the answer is I did not like them.

I hope that we can learn a lesson from these articles; namely, that there are certain things in a corporation that, for the benefit and well-being of each one of the employees and the business as a whole, are best kept within the walls. High on this list are gossip, hearsay, and surmise. When we violate this precaution, individually or as a group, we are weakening the position of the company.

It would be unrealistic to draw too close a comparison between a corporation and a family. There is a similarity, though. In the privacy of our homes, all of us occasionally must grapple with family problems as best we can. In the interest of the family, however, we keep such internal matters to ourselves.

By the same token, I have always believed that it is good business for a company to be united toward the outside world rather than like a group of individuals who are pulling against each other. I don't mean for one minute that we should pull our punches in the house. Healthy criticism is what has built the IBM company in the past and will continue to build it in the future. We all welcome criticism, if we're smart.

The number of queries to me about the *Fortune* articles is an indication of the interest level in the public eye which IBM has reached. This in turn is an indication of how careful each of us must be in our relationships with outside reporters and even with friends outside the company when it comes to discussing matters that are pertinent to and are going on inside the company.

I hope my explaining to each of you my feelings about these articles will help all of us march ahead together and reflect as much credit upon this corporation as possible. I have the highest expectations that all of us can learn our lessons from this and that in the future we will be more sophisticated in how we discuss the internal problems of this company with outsiders.

Thomas J. Watson Jr.

Number 1-67: February 21, 1967

We believe most people in IBM have always considered the company a career, rather than a single stop in a series of jobs. But people do leave IBM to take positions in other companies, many of them talented and experienced people we very much wanted to keep in the business.

Recently we surveyed a number of these ex-IBMers to determine why they had left. One of the most important reasons they gave was their feeling that they had no opportunity for advancement in IBM. They didn't know about opportunities in other locations, in other divisions, in other functions.

How could this happen in a company expanding as rapidly as ours, with 25,000 employees being hired last year alone? The common answer, in the cases of those we surveyed, seems to be that the man's manager didn't do an adequate job of helping him find a job within IBM that would make the best use of his talent and experience. Some managers were unable to provide information about job opportunities and skills needed elsewhere in IBM. But more often, a manager, because of the pressure to get the job done, was reluctant to let go of a good employee. Rather than trying to find him a more responsible spot, the manager seemed to be holding him in his job so he could help the department meet its goals.

One of your most basic responsibilities as managers is developing men. When you are successful, you may develop a man right out of your area and into another part of the business. Fine. Your job is to build talented people not just for your department, but for the IBM company.

We can't afford to lose able people, especially now when the IBM company is expanding so rapidly to meet its commitments. When your good people, whom you have carefully and conscientiously helped develop, are ready to move, make sure they move up, not out.

Thomas J. Watson Jr.

Number 2-67: April 18, 1967

In 1966, IBM employed 25,000 new people worldwide. Thanks in part to the good communications job done by managers, many of these new people are already performing like veterans. Apparently most of you understand that when a person gets a lot of information from his manager, and has a chance to be heard, he usually feels he's part of the team and becomes highly motivated to give the kind of dedicated performance the company needs.

However, if the feedback we get from Speak Up!s, surveys and Open Door cases is reliable, and I think it is, there are still some managers in IBM who are not communicating with their people as effectively as they might. In some situations a manager didn't talk plainly enough or often enough to his people. In others, a manager didn't listen.

In a letter that was published in a recent issue of *IBM News*, I asked all employees to be sure to speak out when they have important things to say about their jobs or the business. But we will get the benefit of their ideas only if we are ready to listen.

Perhaps the most effective way to improve communications is to hold meetings with all of your people – and I mean every one of them no matter what job they are doing. I know that many of you hold operating meetings in your department on a regular basis. But they are no substitute for the kind of employee-manager meetings that I'm talking about, which have quite a different purpose. I hope you will hold meetings with your people in which you clearly demonstrate that you are ready, willing and able to listen to their thoughts and suggestions. Try to produce an exchange of ideas. Don't be discouraged if some of your meetings don't seem to produce much give and take. Opinion surveys, Open Door letters and Speak Up!s show that IBMers have a great many questions to ask and ideas to offer. When they become convinced that your meetings will be regular, that you sincerely want people to talk, and that their questions will be given serious attention, they will speak out.

If we hope to benefit from the ideas and experience that IBMers can offer, it is up to all of us to create an on-the-job atmosphere that says: "Speak out. We're listening."

Thomas J. Watson Jr.

Number 3-67: May 1, 1967

In January 1967, IBM's total employment for the first time exceeded 200,000 people. To retain a "small company" attitude – even as we pass ever larger milestones – we have long made a practice of trying to give managers the authority they need to make as many of their own decisions as possible. This is a good practice and in general it works very well. When decisions can be made where the problem is, the company can turn around faster and can move faster to meet the customer's needs.

But when we make decisions about personnel matters, especially about working conditions, we have to face two significant facts. First, our communications lines are so short that a local decision made in California one day is being discussed in New York the next day. Because word spreads so fast, an individual manager's decision about personnel matters may easily commit some other location to the same action. This creates a snowball effect. For instance, in one laboratory location a fairly unusual exhibit of inventions was placed in the cafeteria. Their function was to attract scientists and not to set any precedent. Later, however, at a plant location, a cafeteria was built with such elegant decor that some of the people who worked there were embarrassed to eat in it.

In another location it was suggested that we put up steel guard rails along a road where no real hazard existed. If they had been put up, we might well have found ourselves with a policy of installing steel guard rails on both sides of every IBM driveway in the world.

The second fact we have to face is that decisions of this sort, about such things as hours of work, safety regulations, parking arrangements and food service, seem to take us down a one-way street. Once we change the hours of work, it is very hard to change them back. Once we add a coffee break, it is very hard to drop it. Such decisions can cause a loss of flexibility throughout the business.

Before any of us makes a decision that may liberalize personnel policies governing work scheduling, food service, and the like, we should review that decision with extreme care to be sure that it is really essential and that it does not have adverse implications for other IBM locations. If any doubts at all exist, the personnel manager should be consulted, so that he may, if necessary, contact the office of the Vice President, Personnel, for advice and guidance.

Thomas J. Watson Jr.

Number 4-67: July 19, 1967

The Open Door Policy is one of our company's most valuable assets. It gives the IBMer who is having trouble on the job a chance to get at least two different people focusing on his problem. It lets the IBM company demonstrate, day in and day out, our belief in fair treatment and respect for the individual.

But you run the risk of turning this asset into a liability if you let the Open Door Policy intimidate you.

I stress this point because there is clearly a tendency among some managers to avoid action on difficult personnel problems if such action might lead to an Open Door case. I think this tendency will diminish if all of you understand what higher management looks for when it reviews such cases.

We try to find out whether the employee has received fair treatment. We want to know if he has been given every reasonable opportunity to know where he stands, to discuss his problems and to improve his performance. We also try to learn whether the manager has given the employee a consistent interpretation of company policy. However, on such matters as assessing the performance of an employee, we try not to second guess the manager. Those judgments are for the manager to make.

What we sometimes find in Open Door cases is that the problems come from the manager's inaction. Unwilling to make a difficult decision, fearful of creating an Open Door case no matter which move he makes, the manager may do nothing. That's the worst mistake he could make. It's usually better to make almost any decision than to make no decision.

Another mistake that some managers make is spending long, valuable hours putting everything about the case down on paper to protect themselves. That's a waste of time. Long memos to the file are not required. All that is needed is simple documentation of the essential points on which the case turns. Any manager who spends excessive amounts of time writing memos and building up a case just to protect himself lacks confidence not only in himself but also in IBM management.

On the whole, IBM managers are doing an excellent job of managing. Clearly, the decisions you make are, by and large, fair and courageous. For example, in a substantial majority of Open Door cases that came to me last year, a review of the facts showed that lower management had made the right decision and their judgment was upheld. I think that if you keep this fact in mind, you will be able to face troublesome personnel problems with less apprehension, and therefore greater fairness – to your employees, to the company, and to yourself.

Thomas J. Watson Jr.

Number 5-67: September 14, 1967

This year marks the fifth anniversary of IBM's participation in the "Plan for Progress" program established by the President's Committee on Equal Employment Opportunity.

As signers, IBM and some 360 other firms which together employ over nine million employees pledged to give all job applicants equal opportunity for employment and equal treatment during employment.

IBM's participation in this government program is an additional commitment to our belief in equal job opportunity for all. Our company pledged itself to this cause many years ago and – thanks to the outstanding efforts of IBM managers at all levels and locations – excellent results have materialized.

In recent months, however, our rate of progress has not been as good as we expected it to be. Because of this, especially in light of the obviously growing national problem, intensified action by IBM is called for. All of us must redouble our efforts, therefore, so we can achieve results of which we can be proud.

In addition to recruiting minority group employees, we must work more aggressively on the long-range intent of the "Plan for Progress" program – to help minority group employees grow in their jobs and advance up the promotional ladder. To do a still better job in achieving this larger objective, we need greater support from every IBM manager.

As a reminder to all of you of the significance of this program, we are attaching a booklet – "IBM Plan for Progress" – issued five years ago. You will profit by a careful reading or re-reading of it.*

We ask that you continue to make IBM's commitment to this vital national cause your own commitment.

*Attachment no longer available

Thomas J. Watson Jr.

Number 6-67: September 29, 1967

In IBM we have always tried to appoint as managers ambitious, hardworking men and women who like to get things done. By and large, we have succeeded and the result is a team of people who are building an unparalleled business record. Some managers seem to believe that they can measure their accomplishments by the size of their budgets. Bigness, as the dinosaur discovered, is not necessarily a measure of excellence. So it is with budgets. Obviously, the test of excellence in IBM is how your achievements, not your budgets, grow.

IBM is an expanding company and many budget increases are necessary to develop new programs. But not all of them are essential; some are the products of bureaucratic thinking. A bureaucrat views a decreased budget or a smaller proposal as a sign of diminishing importance or influence in his role. Or he believes that if he cuts a budget this year, he will find it hard to get new money for an important proposal next year. Or he fears that the money he saves on his budget will be spent elsewhere by some other manager.

Such thinking is illogical. We are all on the same team. A manager who achieves his goal with fewer resources is saving money for all of us. At the same time he is making it possible for the company to make a greater profit and to grow faster. Certainly this benefits every member of the team.

Managers, by an intelligent and realistic approach to the problem, can cut unnecessary costs without cutting output. One manager who increased output without increasing his budget explained his philosophy this way: "I try to get financial management down to the lowest possible level. We get the most out of our money by dividing the responsibility for how we spend it among as many interested people as possible. By making those directly involved a part of the effort, we got areas that were way out of line functioning 40% more efficiently without spending any more money."

Needless to say, he, and other managers like him, got promoted. Men such as this are at a premium. It is optimistic to expect that all managers can boost their output without a corresponding boost in their budget. But I believe that most managers can do it, and those who do can look forward to an especially bright future in this company.

Thomas J. Watson Jr.

Number 7-67: October 6, 1967

Our Appraisal and Counseling Program promises every employee – managers and non-managers – a formal interview with his immediate superior once each year on a scheduled anniversary date. It also promises, obviously, that the appraisal will be done by a superior who, through personal knowledge over a reasonable period of time, is qualified to judge an individual's performance.

These are commitments by IBM to its people. I expect them to be honored without reservation.

I bring this up now because there is increasing evidence that not all of us are meeting our obligations in the Appraisal and Counseling Program. I know of cases where appraisals have been delayed, postponed or put off for weeks with very flimsy excuses; there are also cases where appraisals have been attempted by unqualified persons because the knowledgeable manager had been transferred or promoted and thought he could conveniently avoid this duty.

We all like to give "good" appraisals. When an employee is performing satisfactorily, displays initiative and responsibility and has a good grasp of his career potential, the appraisal interview can be easy and enjoyable. These are usually on time.

But, as managers, we must occasionally face those unpleasant situations where it's not that easy. Perhaps an employee, performing below standards, needs individual guidance; perhaps he needs reassurance on his career with IBM; perhaps, every reasonable effort having been made, an employee must improve or be separated from the business. In these situations it is particularly important that there should be no delay. Postponing it or compromising its quality can only harm the employee and the company.

IBM's dedication to the dignity of the individual is no myth. To me it is the very essence of our success. You were selected to be a manager partly because you displayed a belief in this policy and the ability to carry it out. Appraising and counseling are major parts of your job. They must be done promptly and properly. Nothing less can be tolerated.

Thomas J. Watson Jr.

Number 8-67: October 23, 1967

I keep six honest serving-men
(They taught me all I knew);
Their names are What and Why and When
And How and Where and Who

Rudyard Kipling wrote these lines about sixty-five years ago. But as far as I am concerned, they are fundamental to the responsibility of IBM managers at all levels, today. If these so-called "serving-men" are used with discretion and yet used vigorously, there is almost no managerial job in the corporation that will not be done well.

Let me tell you how I personally apply this Kipling approach. When I visit a headquarters or plant or lab or field office, I try to make the "six honest serving-men" work overtime. If I see dirt on a showroom window or a scratch on the demonstration machine or crumpled paper on the floor or evidence of lateness, I ask why the conditions are permitted and who is doing something about them. Some managers are surprised that I am interested in such apparently minor details, and fortunately the majority of my work is involved in much more major items. However, I think that every IBM manager has an obligation to question practices or decisions that seem to him to be harmful or wasteful in any way whatsoever and his sense of responsibility for these things should extend beyond his own department.

If you and I don't ask these questions, then the dirt will stay on the windows and the machine will get another scratch and the reputation of the IBM company for excellence will suffer. The initial impact is small but there is a snowballing effect. If we don't ask about the cost of the interbuilding bus transportation or about the cost of double – sometimes triple – food service, and so forth, then the money we spend on these things will slowly add up to a staggering amount of waste.

We've always had, in IBM, many managers who are imbued with "the small company attitude" – part of this is a sense of personal responsibility for the company's progress and reputation. Whenever these men and women see a chance to improve the performance or reputation of the company, they act.

As the company grows larger, this sense of personal responsibility becomes more important than ever in keeping the company flexible and responsive. At the same time, it can be frustrated by the very complexity of our expanding operations. The solution, I think, is for each of us to put Kipling's six serving-men to work. If we take the initiative, ask these questions and act on the answers, there is almost no item of importance in the operation of the corporation that will not be attended to promptly.

Thomas J. Watson Jr.

Number 9-67: December 12, 1967

Occasionally I am presented with an Open Door case or a
Speak Up! arising from the same basic question – "I've now received a college degree (or completed some other significant
step in education). Why am I not being promoted?"

These situations are particularly distressing on two counts.
First, the question is based on a misunderstanding that should
never exist; second, even the most careful after-the-fact explanation of policy often leaves the employee feeling frustrated
and betrayed.

I remember one case in which a man put in ten years of
part-time study to earn a college degree, all the while expect-
ing that when he graduated he would automatically be promoted. When the time finally came, he asked to be considered
for a number of jobs, and was interviewed for several. Unfortunately, even with the degree, he wasn't promotable. Eventually
he got a different job – a better one – but he was bitter at what
he thought was a "double-cross."

Let's assume that his managers during those ten years did
their jobs properly to the extent that they knew he was studying
in his spare time and knew he was ambitious for advancement
in the company. What they did not do, apparently, was take
the obvious next step of putting his efforts and his goals in the
proper perspective.

To begin with, every manager should know – and should let
his people know – that in IBM there is no single circumstance
or condition under which a promotion is automatic. Advancement is based primarily on performance in the present job plus
evaluation of his potential by his manager. If the promotion is
to a supervisory position, then we must add such considerations as leadership qualities, administrative abilities and judgment. Education, of any kind, becomes a factor only insofar

as it influences and enhances the abilities and qualities of the person involved.

This is an area that requires most careful and sensitive handling. We must continue to encourage and recognize education for its own merits. But we must never oversell it with an expressed or implied promise of automatic promotion.

Thomas J. Watson Jr.

Number 1-68: March 5, 1968

Our company's success comes in no small part from the way we are organized to work together as a team. But a few recent signs suggest that some managers, especially newer ones, may not understand our present pattern of organization well enough to discuss it with their employees.

In the last few months a number of us have been asked such questions as: Just what divisions are in the DP Group today? Where do the three subsidiaries fit? How do the operating units, such as the divisions and subsidiaries, relate to the corporate staff? What is ASDD's current mission? Or IRD's?

Some of these questions are understandable. Ours is a fast moving business and it's hard to keep up with all aspects of the company's organization. On the other hand, it is important that our people know how their work fits into the company as a whole.

IBM's present organization is described in the attachment.* You should read it carefully to be sure you understand how your unit relates to others in the company. You should also use this material in manager-employee meetings to improve your people's understanding of IBM's organization and their role in it.

---

* A current description of IBM's organization is now contained in the *IBM Manager's Manual.*

Thomas J. Watson Jr.

Number 3-68: May 24, 1968

The attitude persists in many parts of the company that the only way to get ahead is to move. As a consequence, people are being moved too often and for the wrong reasons. We do a disservice to our people and our business when we use relocation as the principal method of placement and career development.

The human costs involved concern me most. I have seen the unpleasant things that can happen when frequent moves disrupt families, complicate financial plans and interrupt children's education. And I know this kind of pressure can hurt a man's personal development and effectiveness on the job.

We could try to solve this problem with excessive rules and restrictions on relocations, but that would take the responsibility for managing people out of your hands – where it rightfully belongs. The best solution lies in a basic change in our attitude toward the placement and development of people.

Our guiding principle must be that we will make only those relocations that are essential to a person's career growth and the health of the business.

Fortunately, IBM today offers more opportunities than ever before to move people up without moving them to new locations. We must look more diligently among local people to fill job openings, and not overplay the real or imagined minor weaknesses that in the past have caused the man on the spot to be overlooked in favor of someone who "looks perfect" – but only from a distance.

Obviously, we will have to continue to relocate some people. But we must be sure that each move is necessary to IBM and an important step in a person's long-term career growth. By observing these requirements we can continue to provide qualified people with rewarding and challenging opportunities while holding relocation situations to a minimum.

Thomas J. Watson Jr.

Number 4-68: June 14, 1968

Last year, employees provided 35,000 savings ideas which helped to offset mounting cost levels in the company. These ideas produced economies worth over $150 million, or more than four percent of total cost and expense outlays. The dollar range varied from $100 to $1.7 million.

This kind of response to our Cost Effectiveness programs is tremendously encouraging. It means that IBMers are not willing, despite our excellent business record, to allow success to divert them from sound business practices and effective decisions about time, money, resources and people.

Equally important, I suspect that wherever we have made savings – whether one hundred dollars or one million dollars – there has been an enthusiastic manager involved, building an atmosphere which motivates his people to seek improvement and economy in everything they do.

More of us should do the same. Cost Effectiveness, as a continuing program, depends almost entirely on your leadership and on your skill in presenting it as a basic concept of good business in which everyone must become involved. I expect each of you to give this the time and attention it requires.

As we grow in size, we must make certain that what we're adding is not excess weight, but healthy muscle.

Thomas J. Watson Jr.

Number 5-68: July 31, 1968

In August, *IBM News* will carry a letter from me urging IBMers in this national election year not only to vote, but also to consider getting involved in the political campaigns now taking place. Employees may have questions concerning the relationship between their political activity and their employment with IBM and to help you in answering these, I want to restate our policies on this subject.

- First of all, we participate in politics as private citizens, not as IBMers. Obviously then, we should not use our company positions to influence, in any way, the political opinions of anyone inside or outside IBM.
- We will grant any employee reasonable amounts of time off without pay to campaign for himself or others. But, because of various federal and state laws, a company cannot pay employees for time off for political activity. We will give people time off with pay to work at the polls during an election because this is not prohibited by law.
- We should not use IBM time, money or materials for political purposes. This includes IBM equipment, stationery, reproduction services and secretarial services.
- When someone from IBM gives a political speech, he should make sure his audience understands that he is speaking as an individual and not as a representative of the company.

Several years ago I also answered some questions about political activity for one of our company publications. I am including here a copy of that interview because I think the answers may be helpful to you in applying our policies.

Political Activity – Guidelines

Q: *Mr. Watson, we have often heard the expression, "business and politics don't mix." What is your opinion on this?*

A: I don't believe that the company should attempt to mobilize its people in the support of any party, person or cause. It should not try to function as a political organization in any way. To that extent, I agree that business and politics don't mix. However, this does not mean that any individual in the corporation should feel restricted from exercising his own political responsibility. The fact that we work for a corporation should have absolutely no bearing whatsoever on whether, or how much, we participate in politics.

Q: *What is the company's policy on politics?*

A: Our policy is to encourage employees to participate in politics to the fullest extent. We will do everything reasonable to accommodate employees who are required to be away from their jobs while running for, or holding, significant office, or while fulfilling significant party duties during a campaign or election. Our encouragement of individual political activity is not tied to parties or issues. It is given on the basis that the primary purpose is to benefit the community, state or country.

Q: *Just what do you mean by "participating in politics"?*

A: I mean participating in any activity at the local, state or national level involving the choice of public officials and the administration of political parties and governmental affairs. This includes, first of all, registering and voting in elections. In addition, if you really want to stand up and be counted, I suggest that you go to your local party headquarters and offer your services. I'm sure they'll have plenty for you to do. There are jobs to fit practically anyone's experience.

Q: *Would political activity help – or hinder – my IBM career?*

A: Well, it certainly would not hinder you. While political activity will not be considered as a factor in promotions, I would think that a man in politics might pick up some good experience that would help him handle his responsibilities in IBM.

Q: *How far can a manager or employee go in expressing his political convictions on the job?*

A: I would say that is largely up to the individual, considering his own position, the propriety of political discussion in a business setting, and the possible effects on customers and subordinates. I would think that ordinary prudence would dictate how far an individual would go in this direction. Specifically, I see nothing wrong about stating a position, or advertising your particular persuasion by wearing campaign buttons or urging others to your point of view, provided such activity does not interfere with your work or the work of others. I would caution any manager to avoid any political discussion that might give the impression he is trying to use his position to influence people who report to him.

Thomas J. Watson Jr.

Number 6-68: August 9, 1968

An employee recently wrote a Speak Up! saying: "I know it is unlikely that we would have a Be-Kind-to-Managers Day, but I think it is time for us non-managerial people to stop and consider just how many problems and responsibilities our managers have.... I would just like to say thank you to my manager, and to managers like him, for caring more than anyone could ask."

I am always glad to get letters like this because they show we are on the right track. In a company growing as rapidly as ours, the need for such rapport between the manager and his people is fundamental.

We can learn from praise, sometimes almost as much as from problems. Here is another tribute, and it tells a lot: "He always has time to listen to anything you have to say.... He is honest, fair and a friend to each of us.... If you have a question, he answers it straight out, no beating around the bush.... The best thing is, you always know where you stand with him...."

This kind of comment gives a clear indication of some of the qualities people feel are important in managers. They are essentially the same qualities we look for first in managers.

Managing people is not a popularity contest, and we are all well aware that there are some decisions which are hard to make and tough to take. But the continued success of our corporation clearly depends on how well managers bring out the energies and talents of their people. If the basic communication between the individual and his manager does not exist, all the other communications devices will not suffice. Our people must respond to one another and, as these letters show, the response begins with your leadership.

Thomas J. Watson Jr.

Number 7-68: August 30, 1968

Last year we hired some 25,000 new people – and in the process we had to turn down several times that number.

This raises a sensitive problem. It is extremely important that unsuccessful applicants go away with the feeling they have been treated fairly and courteously, and that IBM's concern for the individual is a commitment which really means something.

We must be prompt. The company as a whole can maintain a reputation for promptness if each of you as managers develops the habit of expediting applications. For instance, if a referral is appropriate, it should be finalized by telephone rather than by mail, so that the applicant knows immediately – and without vagueness – where and to whom he is being referred.

There are pitfalls. Don't refer an applicant elsewhere unless you really would hire the person if you had a suitable opening. Don't lead applicants to believe they are receiving favorable consideration if, in fact, it is clear to you they will be turned down. They deserve to be told the truth as tactfully and promptly as possible.

And there are certain cases which require extraordinary sensitivity, as when the applicant believes he merits special consideration – for example, widows of IBM employees, sons and daughters of IBMers, and handicapped persons. We do not "make" jobs for these people, and we must hire the best applicants. But where other factors are equal, preferential treatment should be given to such applicants. If we still have to turn them down, and are not sensitive to what they see as their special claims, we can damage our reputation for fairness and courtesy.

All applicants are part of our public. If they don't join us, they may ultimately go to work for one of our customers, or move into any one of a multitude of areas where our good name is constantly at stake. Because they were turned down by us, their encounter with IBM may have been somewhat disappointing – but it need not leave a bitter taste in their mouths if we are careful.

I am not suggesting we should over-compensate when we have to say no. I am simply saying you should extend to these applicants the same courtesy you would expect yourself if the situation were reversed.

Thomas J. Watson Jr.

Number 8-68: September 10, 1968

Suggestions can be looked upon in two ways. One is to regard them as a time-consuming nuisance. The other is to see them as a sincere attempt to improve the business.

The attitude you adopt, as managers, determines how successful the Suggestion Plan will be. And the key is this: prompt and thorough handling of suggestions.

The IBM Suggestion Plan is 40 years old this year. It has proved itself a valuable business asset. In 1967, based on estimated savings to the company of approximately $15 million, we paid out $3.5 million in awards to employees. The dividends come in satisfaction as well as savings, for the Suggestion Plan is a great stimulus to the creativity of IBMers.

This is an excellent record, but it can be improved.

First of all, suggestions must be considered current business. Delays create a backlog, postpone the benefits of good ideas, and make the company look a good deal less responsive than we ask our own people to be.

But promptness alone will not produce the desired results. Each suggestion merits a thorough investigation and an objective evaluation. When a suggestion is adopted, we should be sure the employee receives every appropriate recognition for it. If the idea is not acceptable, the reasons should be made clear in a candid but tactful response.

Remember that behind each suggestion is an IBMer who has put something of himself into the idea, and who is waiting with understandably keen interest for the outcome. Win or lose, he deserves a prompt, fair and understandable answer.

Thomas J. Watson Jr.

Number 9-68: October 25, 1968

In IBM, we have made progress in our commitment to equal opportunity for all, but the crisis the nation faces in race relations today demands that we make good on that pledge to the fullest extent with the least delay. We have, in fact, much more to do.

Let there be no doubt about our commitment. We are committed not just to statistical compliance with federal law, but to overcoming discrimination throughout our operation, whether in hiring or promoting. There must be no second-class citizens in IBM.

This requires that we evaluate job applicants not just on their past but on their potential. We must look less exclusively at the individual's education, work experience, references and record, and more readily at his determination and willingness to learn.

We must look, in short, for ways of fitting people in rather than screening them out. In some cases this requires special training, both before and after hiring.

It is not nearly enough just to hire a minority group employee. You, as a manager, must help him earn the right to progress to bigger responsibilities and higher pay. Our goal is that a member of a minority group should know he has the same chance for progress as does any other IBMer – not a *better* chance, but an *equal* chance.

IBM has become what it is by dealing with its people on an individual basis, judging a man's value to the company strictly on his merit.

The challenge now – and it is a high priority task – is to bring this idea to full and convincing life for all, regardless of race or color.

Thomas J. Watson Jr.

Number 10-68: November 26, 1968

An IBMer in Boulder wrote to me recently suggesting that we change THINK, the company slogan, to COMMUNICATE. His argument is that many of our day-to-day problems can be traced back to a communications breakdown.

He makes an excellent point. The THINK slogan is as valid as ever and we do not plan to change it – but unless thinking results in effective communication, and then action, we are doing only half the job. I wonder how many good ideas have been lost because the thinker could not aptly communicate his idea, or – equally important – because the other person wasn't listening.

The symptoms of poor communication are false starts, wrong conclusions, poor morale. We cannot afford them. You as a manager can establish the habit of good communication in your area if you will encourage your people to develop good ideas, help them bring problems into focus, and insist on clarity. Just to listen is not enough.

I'll give you an example. Studies have shown that too many IBMers do not understand the career paths open to them. Here is a failure to communicate. You can help tackle it by discussing opportunities with your personnel department and your management, and developing appropriate career paths. It is not always possible to set them down like routes on a map, for many situations are unique, but in some divisions there are publications like DPD's "Guidelines for Career Opportunities" to help you. The point is that effective communication begins with an informed and understanding manager.

Then there is the problem of gobbledygook. One of the ironies of our business is that we can transmit the most complex information in a fraction of a second with the computer – but when we use the written or spoken word to communicate with one another in everyday situations, we often fall back on jargon which obscures our meaning. We put long words where short ones will serve, fancy phrases where plain talk is needed.

My father used to urge people to "talk net," and he had the right idea. He meant cut out the verbiage, and get down to business. I think this was in part what the writer in Boulder had in mind.

In a business that moves as fast as ours, that is as complex as ours, that has as many people as ours, good communications is our lifeblood. Listen to your people. Talk to them. Not just now and then. But often, as a way of life.

Thomas J. Watson Jr.

Number 11-68: December 30, 1968

Most IBMers know and observe the basic rule that we don't knock the competition. We don't disparage his products, his people or his services.

But sometimes, without meaning to, we can violate this rule. We can be misunderstood when we say something about our competition because of how we say it or to whom we say it.

For instance, during a talk at a professional meeting, one of our people was asked for his personal appraisal of a product that could be construed as competitive. Unfortunately, even though he had made it clear that the opinion was his own, his critical remarks were construed by some people as a deliberate IBM disparagement of a competitor's product.

How can we avoid these situations? Certainly there are times when we have to express opinions. Customers ask questions. Prospects want to know what we think. We have to participate in industry and professional activities, exchange ideas, share knowledge and learn from others. But we can eliminate some of the problems if we bear in mind that, whatever we say, how it sounds to our listeners often depends on the occasion – the time, the place, the audience and the subject.

We certainly don't want to impose a gag rule on anyone. I want our people to speak out when they are called upon for their ideas, both inside and outside IBM. I am willing to accept occasional corporate embarrassment rather than shut off the expression of opinion. But, we must use judgment and common sense in what we say.

We don't want to damage any company's reputation. We can do business very well without that. We always have. And we always will depend for our success upon the excellence of our own products, our own services, our own people. That's basic.

Thomas J. Watson Jr.

Number 1-69: January 30, 1969

In IBM the manager's word must be believable. Therefore, if he makes a commitment to an employee, that commitment should not be overruled by a more senior manager without very careful deliberation, and then only in rare circumstances.

We have had situations recently which underline the importance of this. One employee who had poorly handled a customer call was counseled by his first line manager but told he could stay on the job. A senior manager, when he reviewed the decision, felt the offense was more serious – and dismissed the employee. A trainee was told by his first line manager that he had three weeks to improve his class grades or he would be separated from the business; when this decision was reviewed by the next level of management the probationary period was arbitrarily reduced to one week.

In other situations, people have been led to believe they were going to get certain jobs, promotions, or opportunities. They have made their plans and preparations, only to find the rug pulled out from under them by "a decision from higher up."

Clearly, this sort of thing can undermine authority and create a great deal of disappointment and confusion.

To avoid getting locked into situations like this, the immediate manager should check with his own manager on unusually sensitive problems before making a final decision. If the circumstances warrant, the first manager must be prepared to defend both his own convictions and the employee he represents.

In the end, he may still be overruled, for there are times when it is the senior manager's duty to overrule him – but not until the employee's manager is satisfied that the situation is fully understood. Similarly, the senior manager must avoid reversing a commitment unless he fully understands the situation, and the circumstances are such that a reversal is warranted.

Confidence in a manager's commitment to the employee is one of the cornerstones on which this company is built, and that confidence must be sustained. Remember that the immediate manager is the employee's first line of defense as well as counsel.

Thomas J. Watson Jr.

Number 2-69: February 12, 1969

Almost ten years ago, we began the Speak Up! program as an experiment to give our people an added way to ask questions, to complain, or just to be heard.

Since then, the program has brought us over 50,000 letters. Today, we are answering about 10,000 a year. I personally see a number of these and I review the entire program regularly. From my experience, I would say that most employees like having Speak Up! around.

Some of our managers, however, may think of the program as a threat – a device which encourages your people to go over your head with petty gripes. For instance, I heard about one manager who actually tried to intercept a Speak Up! when he saw an employee drop it in the outgoing mail. He told the man, in effect, that if he had anything to complain about, he should complain to him, his manager.

Our continuing aim, of course, is that an employee's manager will always be his primary source of information. But there are several reasons an employee might not want to go to him directly.

In some cases, an IBMer uses Speak Up! because he doesn't think his manager would have the information he wants, such as a detailed explanation of why we don't market a certain widget.

In other cases, an employee might be reluctant to approach his manager with a complaint on some situation, such as parking space, either because his manager is not directly responsible for it, or he doesn't want to appear to be a chronic griper.

In still other cases, the IBMer may feel that he can't communicate directly with his manager because the manager has been unresponsive or insensitive to his needs in the past. In this situation, Speak Up! is the sort of safety valve we simply must have.

But Speak Up! is not just a vehicle for employee complaints; it is meant to help you communicate better with your people – to listen better, to answer better.

If you read the Speak Up! column in the IBM employee publications, you can find out what employees are concerned about, and how insensitive managerial attitudes and actions affect morale. Look and listen for similar problems in your own area and examine your own performance.

If you should be called upon to answer a Speak Up! question, answer it frankly. Bureaucratic answers and fuzzy evasions just won't do.

You may feel impelled to write a Speak Up! yourself. By all means do so, if you need to.

Speak Up! is not intended to be the whole answer to our communications problems. But it is a highly useful medium in itself, and if we will use it, it can help us become better informed, more responsive, and therefore more effective managers.

Thomas J. Watson Jr.

Number 3-69: April 7, 1969

As you all know, we have long held to three basic beliefs in the conduct of this business: Respect for the individual, the best customer service, and superior accomplishment of all tasks.

These beliefs, combined with IBM management principles, express the goals we seek, the means we use to achieve them, and the obligations we accept along the way.

These ideas don't change. We mean to keep them and we mean to live by them.

Because we have grown so fast in the past few years and because we have so many new managers, I thought it would be well for us to reissue the statement of our beliefs and principles. It last appeared in *Management Briefing* back in 1965.

In reissuing this document, we have combined the basic beliefs and the management principles into one compact statement, but the three basic beliefs – in the individual, in service, and in excellence – retain a special place and a special significance. They are the ones that provide every IBMer, whatever his job, daily guidance in his work and in his relationships with other IBMers and customers.

I hope you will study these principles, know them well, and discuss them with the people you manage.

Basic Concepts - IBM Principles

An organization, like an individual, must build on a bedrock of sound beliefs if it is to survive and succeed. It must stand by these beliefs in conducting its business. Every manager must live by these beliefs in the actions he takes and in the decisions he makes.

The beliefs that guide IBM activities are expressed as IBM Principles.

Respect for the Individual

Our basic belief is respect for the individual, for his rights and dignity. It follows from this principle that IBM should:

- Help each employee to develop his potential and make the best use of his abilities.
- Pay and promote on merit.
- Maintain two-way communications between manager and employee, with opportunity for a fair hearing and equitable settlement of disagreements.

Service to the Customer

We are dedicated to giving our customers the best possible service. Our products and services bring profits only to the degree that they serve the customer and satisfy his needs. This demands that we:

- Know our customers' needs, and help them anticipate future needs.
- Help customers use our products and services in the best possible way.
- Provide superior equipment maintenance and supporting services.

Excellence Must Be a Way of Life

We want IBM to be known for its excellence. Therefore, we believe that every task, in every part of the business, should be performed in a superior manner and to the best of our ability. Nothing should be left to chance in our pursuit of excellence. For example, we must:

- Lead in new developments.
- Be aware of advances made by others, better them where we can, or be willing to adopt them whenever they fit our needs.
- Produce quality products of the most advanced design and at the lowest possible cost.

Managers Must Lead Effectively

Our success depends on intelligent and aggressive management which is sensitive to the need for making an enthusiastic partner of every individual in the organization. This requires that managers:

- Provide the kind of leadership that will motivate employees to do their jobs in a superior way.
- Meet frequently with all their people.
- Have the courage to question decisions and policies; have the vision to see the needs of the company as well as the division and department.
- Plan for the future by keeping an open mind to new ideas, whatever the source.

Obligations to Stockholders

IBM has obligations to its stockholders, whose capital has created our jobs. These require us to:

- Take care of the property our stockholders have entrusted to us.
- Provide an attractive return on invested capital.
- Exploit opportunities for continuing profitable growth.

Fair Deal for the Supplier

We want to deal fairly and impartially with suppliers of goods and services. We should:

- Select suppliers according to the quality of their products or services, their general reliability and competitiveness of price.
- Recognize the legitimate interests of both supplier and IBM when negotiating a contract; administer such contracts in good faith.
- Avoid suppliers becoming unduly dependent on IBM.

IBM Should Be a Good Corporate Citizen

We accept our responsibilities as a corporate citizen in community, national and world affairs; we serve our interests best when we serve the public interest. We believe that the immediate and long-term public interest is best served by a system of competing enterprises. Therefore, we believe we should compete vigorously, but in a spirit of fair play, with respect for our competitors, and with respect for the law. In communities where IBM facilities are located, we do our utmost to help create an environment in which people want to work and live. We acknowledge our obligation as a business institution to help improve the quality of the society we are part of. We want to be in the forefront of those companies which are working to make our world a better place.

Thomas J. Watson Jr.

Number 4-69: April 16, 1969

A few weeks ago I received a letter signed only "A Proud IBM Secretary." In it she suggested that a *Management Briefing* would be a good way for me to express my views regarding the importance of the IBM secretary.

"The IBM Secretary," she wrote, "should have more status – that means all of us, not just the few in the top echelon. We all do our job – big or small – and if we do it well, our efforts should be appreciated, and we shouldn't be taken for granted. We are hand-picked to serve this great company, and we should be treated so."

Certainly my views agree with hers, and I would like to thank this secretary for bringing her thoughts to my attention. I would just go one step further, however, and broaden the perspective to include all IBM employees.

It seems to me that the central point of this letter – personal appreciation – is the very essence of good management and the distinguishing mark of a good manager. For while the IBM company can reward employees materially in the form of good pay and benefits, it cannot, as an impersonal entity, express the sincere, spontaneous "Thanks" or "Well done" that all of us from time to time need. That's our job – yours and mine.

If some of us are guilty of taking secretaries for granted, it could be that we are also guilty of taking other employees for granted as well.

Each of us must periodically stop to remember how important personal appreciation and recognition are to every person. Only you are in the spot to recognize a sincere effort or an honest try, and only you can reward it in this most meaningful way.

Thomas J. Watson Jr.

Number 5-69: April 25, 1969

An IBMer suggests we avoid setting unrealistic deadlines. He writes that morale gets undermined if target dates turn out to be phony. I agree.

Most of us have been guilty at one time or another of imposing a deadline ahead of when it was really necessary. The early date provides a cushion against crises, and makes us look good if we can deliver before schedule.

But we pay a price for such luxuries. If a project goes through the chain of command, with each manager demanding an especially early delivery date, the deadline soon becomes yesterday. The person at the end of the chain is placed in a tough spot, and the whole project is likely to suffer from a bad start. Cynicism sets in.

Don't let this happen. Don't put your people on the hot seat just to give yourselves a comfortable cushion.

We pride ourselves in IBM on fast response to customer needs, or to emergencies. We must always be ready to respond with maximum effort. But like everything else, this can be overdone. Speed becomes an end in itself. Judgment goes out of the window.

If we cry wolf when it is not necessary, when the real crisis comes there may be no one listening. Let's not demoralize people with false alarms.

Thomas J. Watson Jr.

Number 6-69: May 13, 1969

Not too long ago, someone outside the company asked me why
we had a policy against buying unsolicited photographs from
outsiders. He was told this when he offered one of our locations some photographs he had taken of a new IBM building
near his home. A little checking showed that our people were
ducking the issue. They had examined the pictures, found
them of poor quality, but had been afraid to say so, because
the neighbor might go away mad. So they invented a "policy":
"We don't use unsolicited photos." He went away mad anyway,
annoyed at this silly, bureaucratic answer.

In another case, one of our college recruiters was told
by a student that he wouldn't work for us if we were the last
company on earth. It seems that a few months before he
had been rejected as a programmer trainee by another IBM
recruiter because he lacked a degree in mathematics, which
our "policy" required.

Of course, there is no such policy, as this unhappy young
student had later found out. He had been rejected because our
recruiter thought the student was not seriously interested in an
IBM career. The recruiter should have told him so, instead of
hiding behind the smokescreen of a non-existent policy.

In our business lives, we often have to say "no," and how
we do it is very important.

The right way, of course, is to make the "no" clear, with
a courteous explanation of why the proposal or the request
is not acceptable.

The wrong way is to be evasive, or to invent an instant
policy that says it can't be done, as a means of softening
the rejection.

With a little thought, all of us, when we have to reject an
idea or a proposal can do it with tact and honesty.

Thomas J. Watson Jr.

Number 7-69: June 11, 1969

There's a special regard, both inside and outside the company, for IBM managers. One of the reasons for this is the thorough and complete way our managers live up to their positions of trust and responsibility. When managers make mistakes, they are rarely ones of integrity and honesty.

Because of this, I find myself terribly disturbed by a recent situation where a manager knowingly falsified an official document of the company in order to get around an accounting error. Because his intent was to right an inaccuracy and the end result did not cheat the company, he saw nothing wrong with the means used.

I couldn't be in greater disagreement with his thinking. This manager backed away from his responsibility to properly correct a wrong situation and violated the basic foundation of trust on which this business is built. This particular incident related to adjusting an employee's time card, but the issue is broader than that. Reporting the truth – without shortcuts for any reason – must be part and parcel of every manager's thinking. When he okays a company document, this sign-off carries with it agreement that what is presented is, to the best of his knowledge, honest data.

We can't afford management thinking that etches away the fundamental integrity of IBM. Sometimes it takes unusual patience and fortitude to correct areas of the business that need correcting, but under no circumstances can we tolerate a thought process that sees the knowing falsification of an official document as a way to right a wrong.

Thomas J. Watson Jr.

Number 8-69: July 18, 1969

An IBMer sent me a reprint of an article on bringing out
the creativity in people. He felt it would be useful reading
for managers. Our opinion surveys, Speak Up!s, executive
interviews and other listening programs bear him out.
There are persistent complaints of stifled initiative and
ideas that are stillborn.

The complaints are not dominant. In one fairly typical
questionnaire, some IBMers were asked if their managers
tried to make constructive use of ideas concerning job related
matters. Twenty-one percent said "always," 45 said "usually,"
24 percent said "sometimes." Only eight percent said "seldom"
and only two percent said "never."

But that negative 10 percent is too much, and that 24
percent "sometimes" response needs improvement. In IBM,
fostering creativity has got to be everyone's business, and I had
this brought personally home by a recent experience.

A dedicated executive came into my office at the end
of what had seemed to be quite a long day. He made some
suggestions about an area of the business I thought was going
reasonably well. He said that without the change he had in
mind, that segment of IBM would begin to deteriorate.
Because I was frustrated and tired, I gave him a very short
interview and a non-sympathetic rebuff.

Later that evening, I began to worry about the area which
he had pointed out, and by morning had realized that at least
constructive and appropriate attention to his idea would be the
minimum he should expect from me. Therefore, I called him
on the phone, and we talked again. The impact this made on
me was that a pretty good critique on whether or not I am
giving creative people the hearing they deserve is to begin
with the thought, "Obviously, this suggestion is being made
because the man is interested in IBM. If this is his attitude, then

I must have the same interest when I hear him out."

There's an old saying that when you talk – you teach, when you listen – you learn. There are a lot of ideas worth listening to in this company. Let's be sure we're paying attention – we are never so rich in ideas that we can afford not to.

Thomas J. Watson Jr.

Number 9-69: August 26, 1969

In an earlier *Management Briefing* I have discussed the problems that can arise from personal investments. There are generally two kinds of investments which could cause problems:

– The conflict of interest investment that might appear to interfere with the independent exercise of the employee's judgment in the best interest of IBM.

– The "inside" investment, either buying or selling, based on information obtained on the job and not available to all investors.

The American business scene is constantly changing. Our June 23rd announcement changed the way IBM does business. Other companies also, from time to time, modify their operations or add to their product line. In this atmosphere of changing business relationships, it is important that each of us continually reexamines his investments to avoid unknowingly becoming involved in a conflict of interest where none previously existed.

Also, a number of new enterprises have been organized to develop products or services competitive with IBM. Some of these companies are located near IBM facilities and have former IBMers in key positions of management. In some cases, we believe they are using know-how developed by IBM. In special circumstances like these, any investment at all by IBM professional or management people, or by their immediate families, could raise questions of business ethics.

There is no way to state a rule that will apply in all cases. Good and reasonable judgment is the best guide. In the end, it's the responsibility of each individual to avoid a conflict of interest.

Thomas J. Watson Jr.

Number 11-69: December 2, 1969

Young people come to us in great numbers these days. More than half the 22,000 people we hired last year were under 25. They come with new attitudes, new expectations and new ideals. They want to change things for the better.

If we want to lead people like this, we must demonstrate that we do not fear change, but welcome it as a way of life. The truth is, few institutions are more radical than the truly dynamic business corporation. Change is its lifeblood. Most great companies change as they grow – or else they do not long survive.

Yet in the contacts we have with young people, we find many of them do not perceive change as a dynamic factor in business. Too often they don't see beyond the web of rules and jargon that characterizes large organizations. They don't see us responding to the needs of our age.

As managers, our attitude toward such newcomers can make a big difference. If a new employee comes through with an idea, don't just tell him we've looked at that before and rejected it. Circumstances may have changed. The new employee may have new factors or a different approach. It is our job always to be on the lookout for ideas that can be developed into constructive change.

Except for the basic beliefs, we are prepared to change almost everything about this company. This is the message we need to get across to the new generation. Your attitude will tell the story better than my words.

Thomas J. Watson Jr.

Number 1-70: January 26, 1970

Outside or inside the business, the matter of "calendar integrity" is an inherent indication of the orderliness with which the company plans and executes its functions.

When an IBM manager makes an appointment or calls a meeting, he has a responsibility to keep the appointed time.

Probably most of us are well aware of our image in this regard with the external business community and conduct our activities there in a timely manner. But many times, inside the company, we violate this sound business practice and common courtesy. It happens often enough to have prompted one manager in the Data Processing Division to write to me suggesting a *Management Briefing* on the subject if I agree. I certainly do.

To keep people waiting beyond their scheduled appointment is, in most cases, inexcusable. To have people arrive at your office from another IBM location and then inform them you're behind schedule, or that the meeting has been cancelled, is not only inconsiderate but a total waste of valuable time and resource – a luxury that IBM cannot afford.

There is a very negative effect on morale if you ask someone to prepare a presentation for you or your staff and then cancel the time. Most of our employees and managers are dedicated to doing a quality job. After they've "gotten up" for a presentation, the letdown from a cancellation is disheartening, and the "next time" it may not be done as enthusiastically.

The higher in management one moves, the more aware of this problem he must become because of the domino effect that takes place when a change at the top ripples downward. The man at the end of the chain has little or no chance to plan and do his job effectively.

In a business that moves as fast as ours, that is as complex as ours, that has as many people as ours, there will always be the requirement for many meetings, presentations and appointments, but I think we can make "calendar integrity" a way of doing business and benefit from its discipline.

Thomas J. Watson Jr.

Number 2-70: February 19, 1970

A foreign language has been creeping into many of the presentations I hear and the memos I read. It adds nothing to a message but noise, and I want your help in stamping it out. It's called gobbledygook.

There's no shortage of examples. Nothing seems to get finished anymore – it gets "finalized." Things don't happen at the same time but "coincident with this action." Believe it or not, people will talk about taking a "commitment position" and then because of the "volatility of schedule changes" they will "decommit" so that our "posture vis-à-vis some data base that needs a sizing will be able to enhance competitive positions."

That's gobbledygook.

It may be acceptable among bureaucrats but not in this company. IBM wasn't built with fuzzy ideas and pretentious language. IBM was built with clear thinking and plain talk. Let's keep it that way.

Thomas J. Watson Jr.

IBMers have always thrived on solving problems. Whether working in the customer's office, on the production line or in the laboratory, we have tried to look at problems as opportunities in disguise – opportunities to satisfy the customer, improve our skills and make the business grow. I hope IBM people never lose this characteristic.

At the same time, we have always tried to remember that people provide the solutions. We should never become so preoccupied with solving problems that we forget the contributions of people.

For the manager, this means putting the individual first. When your people do a good job, promptly tell them so. The phone call, the letter of appreciation, the personal "thank you" – these day-by-day relationships are the heart and soul of our business. Golden Circles, Hundred Percent Clubs, Outstanding Contribution Awards are important, but they are no substitute for telling someone, in your own personal terms, that he has done a first-rate job and you appreciate it.

Money and title alone are not enough to satisfy the kinds of people that make IBM great. What counts most of all is the knowledge that individual contributions are recognized and valued. We all want to receive that sort of recognition, and we must all be quick to give it, too. I believe you'll find, in most cases, that if you give thoughtful care to your people, they can take care of the problems.

Thomas J. Watson Jr.

Number 4-70: April 14, 1970

IBM and its people have always felt a responsibility for leadership and civic participation in the communities where we live and work. Today, our society is in deeper need than ever before and all of us must live up to that responsibility.

Our products are helping to make dramatic contributions in many areas. IBM as a corporation is contributing through programs of varying nature around the country. But IBM's greatest resource is IBMers. They are where the problems are and they can do the most to help.

We can't, of course, turn large numbers of IBM people loose, on a full-time basis or anything like it, to work on those problems. Our first responsibility is still to make a profit, for if we fail in that, we won't survive to make *any* contribution to society.

What we *can* do, however, is give new attention to an existing practice which permits employees reasonable time off for community activities.

In the months ahead we're going to have many more IBM employees than we do now; and all of our people are going to be increasingly concerned about the shape and direction of society. As a result, IBM managers at every level, in every function and division, are likely to be approached by employees for time off to serve vital community causes.

When an IBMer does identify a community need, feels he can uniquely help to meet that need and cannot do so adequately after working hours, please give his request for time off the benefit of your most careful consideration and judgment.

Thomas J. Watson Jr.

Number 5-70: May 20, 1970

Lately I've heard some comments that make me feel a few
people are letting bigness distort their sense of values: They
make it an excuse to dismiss important things as being *relatively*
small. I have in mind situations such as these:

– A person, during a discussion involving more than a million
dollars of potential revenue, comments that "... this is of
relative unimportance to IBM since we are a seven billion
dollar business."
– A study of expense management that brings on the remark:
"Why get excited over a $100,000 phone bill when it is a
fraction of one percent of our total budget?"
– A production schedule for electronic components is missed
by 500,000 modules, and it's shrugged off as trivial in comparison to annual shipments.

These are exceptional cases – but I doubt that they are
unique. So I want every manager to consider carefully whether
this kind of thinking – this attitude – is influencing him or his
people and, if it is, to take steps to change it.

Keep in mind that we reached an annual revenue of
$7 billion by paying attention to detail and by operating on the
premise that every penny counts. No matter how big we get,
that will always be true, and we must never forget it.

Thomas J. Watson Jr.

Number 6-70: July 21, 1970

An IBM manager shapes each employee's career by the way he appraises, counsels, rewards and disciplines. This is a heavy responsibility that requires sensitivity, thoughtfulness and occasionally great self-control.

When an employee is unreasonable, any manager may be tempted to respond in kind. But an employee's career may hang in the balance, and the manager simply cannot allow himself to act in anger.

Not too long ago, a manager's angry reaction almost cost a man his job. The man was an adequate performer, but he had been simmering over a number of job frustrations. Without an apparent explanation, he began an abusive argument with his manager, who, in a similar burst of anger, fired him. After an investigation, the employee was rehired, not because he was right, but because the manager was wrong.

The situation went out of control when the manager lost his composure. He should have let the man express his feelings and then made it clear that he was prepared to discuss the problem when the employee was ready for a calm and reasonable exchange.

I want to support all IBM managers, and I do when I find their actions were based on reason and on careful consideration of what is best for the employee and the company. But when a manager "blows up" in the face of a problem, he's no longer managing; he has become part of the problem.

Thomas J. Watson Jr.

Number 7-70: August 18, 1970

This month marks the fiftieth anniversary of the Women's Suffrage Movement, and yet securing other equal rights for women is still a national social issue.

Today, in the United States, over 25,000 IBMers – more than 15 percent of the company – are women. Over the past five years, a period of rapid growth for the company, the number of women in professional and management positions has grown more than twice as fast as the company itself. However, women are still disproportionately outnumbered in management and in certain other key jobs.

We are doing some things to change that. We are trying to recruit more women for professional jobs in marketing, engineering, programming, and other areas, and we also have a number of programs under way to identify and promote women who have management potential.

But policies and programs don't address the real problem: the unspoken, often unrealized attitudes of individual managers. Look at your own attitudes; you might discover you have one of these notions about women in business:

–   They lack ambition.
–   They aren't competitive.
–   They fold under pressure.
–   They are good at details but not at handling bigger issues.
–   Their emotions overrule their judgment.
–   They can't supervise men.
–   They can't supervise women.

Any one of these judgments might apply to any woman – or any man. They apply to women as a group only in folklore.

That folklore has no place in IBM. It undercuts our belief in the individual and our commitment to pay and promote on the basis of performance and merit. It wastes precious human resources that we need to keep this business growing and successful. The facts are that when any IBMer is denied a chance to give his – or her – best, the company and all of us in it are the losers. That is a loss we can't afford and must not accept.

Thomas J. Watson Jr.

Number 8-70: October 26, 1970

Some of the most serious management mistakes are made with the best intentions.

Recently, a manager was conducting an appraisal interview with an employee who merited a promotion. With the best intentions, the manager said that a promotion was in store for him within the next 60 or 90 days. Psychologically, the employee and his family began to plan for his advancement.

A few weeks passed, and when nothing had transpired, the employee asked about his situation. His manager, again with good intentions, told him about a possible overseas assignment. When that fell through, the manager tried to cushion the disappointment by describing still another possibility he was pursuing, which unfortunately also fell through.

You can imagine what was happening to the employee. His family was growing insecure, and a gnawing "What's wrong with me?" feeling was growing in him, along with disillusionment with his company. By the time a new assignment was found, the employee and his family had gone through an unnecessary period of anxiety and uncertainty.

All of us are tempted to say too much at times. A manager must level with his people – realistically telling them where they stand and what they can expect. But if he creates false expectations and raises hopes that may have to be dashed, he has become a "promises, promises" manager. And, good intentions never make up for bad judgment.

Thomas J. Watson Jr.

Number 9-70: November 16, 1970

Recently an IBMer wrote me about a poster in a government building that was offensive to him. He also wrote a letter of complaint to a local official – on IBM stationery. The official replied to IBM, asking if we had decided to set the standards for what may or may not be displayed in public buildings in the United States. As an individual citizen, the employee had a good point to make, but by using an IBM letterhead he raised a completely different issue.

In other instances, employees have identified themselves with IBM when they complained about bad service received as individuals, or when writing local government agencies and newspaper editors about political matters, such as zoning applications and school taxes. While these are perfectly appropriate issues for employees, acting as individuals, the situation becomes confused and embarrassing to all concerned when it looks as though the IBM Company is taking a position on the problem at hand.

You should encourage your people to act on their convictions and to speak out when they see something wrong, but make sure they understand the distinction between speaking out as concerned individuals and as IBM spokesmen.

Thomas J. Watson Jr.

Number 1-71: January 12, 1971

Recently an IBMer wrote me about a statement made by a manager at his location: "I only have five years to go for early retirement, and so I'm not going to rock any boats."

I suppose that manager thinks he is protecting himself; actually, he has only stuck his head in the sand, and this is a most vulnerable position.

A few years ago I wrote a *Management Briefing* about "playing it safe." The point is simple, but it is worth restating because it applies more than ever in today's fast-moving business environment. The manager who takes unnecessary risks is foolish, but the manager who tries to avoid necessary risk is just not doing the job of management.

Perhaps the manager who said he was not rocking any boats was only reacting to a moment of frustration; all of us have them. But as the letter I received makes only too clear, a manager's impulsive remark may have consequences that persist long after the moment that prompted it.

As a manager, virtually everything you say and do affects your people. You either enhance their enthusiasm or dampen it, recognize and reward their initiative or discourage it, expand their perceptions or limit them. Leadership is a demanding job that requires continuous awareness; as a manager, that job is yours.

Thomas J. Watson Jr.

Number 2-71: March 26, 1971

My associates, without exception, have told me that I should never write to you about business attire or personal appearance because my comments would be subject to misinterpretation and run the risk of appearing arbitrary. But I have noticed a trend recently which, if not corrected, could eventually affect the performance of this corporation in a negative way, and having been around IBM for nearly 34 years now without having had much success with indirect approaches, I am going to tell you candidly about my concern and ask your help in getting us back on the right track.

I think that too many of our people are beginning to exceed the bounds of good common sense in their business attire.

Whether we like it or not, what we wear to work and how we look on the job does affect our business. In the final analysis, our success is dependent on our customers and prospects electing to use our products and services over those of a competitor. In that sense, the primary business objective of every employee in every job, in every division of the IBM Corporation is to overcome the reasons, whatever they are, that a potential customer may have for not doing business with us. This simply means that we are all salesmen – both individually and collectively. To be successful, our selling must be directed to decision-making business executives, those key individuals in a position to commit their company's assets based on our recommendations, and this is where I think we're beginning to get off the beam in matters of business appearance.

By far, the majority of the top business executives across the country – and I purposefully have held up this communication until I was able to confirm this – still dress in a manner that would, on balance, be described as conservative. Although I will be the first to admit that what is considered conservative is constantly changing and being influenced by new fashions and styles of appearance, I do think it is safe to say that the midstream of executive appearance is generally far behind the leading edge of fashion change.

It stands to reason that these executives dress this way because they personally consider it the most appropriate for conducting their business. It further stands to reason that a salesman who dresses in a similar conservative style will offer little distraction from the main points of business discussion and will be more in tune with the thinking of the executive. Although the logic of this reasoning appeals most obviously to those whose job functions call for direct contact with customer personnel, a similar businesslike appearance reflected by those employees whom a potential customer might casually observe in a plant visit, at a headquarters location, or merely leaving an IBM building after work, can equally influence his thinking.

In simple terms, this is why we have always had a custom of conservative appearance in IBM. It made sense in the past and continues to make sense now, as a marketing tool, just like a plant tour, a customer executive school, or a reputation for excellence.

So what does all this mean? For good business reasons, we do ask our people to come to work appropriately dressed for their job environment. As managers, I would expect you to set the proper example for your people. Each of you has the responsibility to establish and enforce conservative dress and appearance standards consistent with our business objectives.

I know it would make your job easier if we were to issue a set of specific appearance guidelines applicable to the entire company, but I have no intention of ever doing this because it would be both impossible and inappropriate. Rather, as managers of this corporation, I look to each of you to apply your individual judgment – as you do in carrying out many other responsibilities – to help control what appears to be a potential business problem.

T. Vincent Learson

Briefings 3-71 through 2-72
1971 – 1972

T. Vincent Learson

Number 3-71: July 28, 1971

This initial *Briefing* couldn't be on any other subject but people – IBM people. For 36 years I have worked with – and depended on, more times than I can remember – IBMers at every level and in every area of the business. The response, the enthusiasm and the ability have always been there.

IBMers give us this kind of support for a variety of reasons but, I believe, primarily because we respect our people, treat them as individuals, and make their well-being a basic part of our management concern. Today, more than ever, we must continue and strengthen this kind of relationship.

You know as well as I that these are difficult times for IBM. The fact that this is a temporary situation – although when it will end we do not know – hardly eases the apprehension of employees who see things happening that they have not experienced before. They are being asked to work harder at a time when budgets are tight and promotion opportunities are fewer. Many are being inconvenienced by being asked to take different jobs or to relocate.

All of these things are necessary. How well they are accomplished depends almost totally on you. These times demand extraordinary efforts and ingenuity, extraordinary patience and sensitivity in working with people.

The success of IBM always has been and will be based on its people. They have amply demonstrated their willingness to devote all their talents and skills to *their* company. You and I owe them skilled, understanding leadership for this is a proud, hard-hitting team – the best in the world – and we must keep it that way.

T. Vincent Learson

Number 4-71: September 13, 1971

In any large organization there is always the temptation to "play it safe," to duck the tough issues and the difficult decisions, to let someone farther up the line call the shots. I want IBM to be different. Buck-passing means delay and uncertainty, neither of which can we tolerate in a business environment that demands innovation and responsiveness.

The consequences of buck-passing and "playing-it-safe" were brought home recently when an engineer came to me, out of sheer frustration, with a proposal he had made to his management almost a year and a half before. He was asking for a simple "yes" or "no" on something that was still unresolved after all that time.

I asked that a prompt decision be made, and, as it turned out, the engineer received a go-ahead. But clearly, the issue should have been decided much quicker and much farther down in the business. The decision was a close one, and a lot of people simply ducked it. They passed it back for more staff work, or shuffled it off to another department, hoping, apparently, that someone would make the decision for them.

I hope this was an isolated case. But the lessons are clear. A decision deferred is an opportunity lost. In this instance a "yes" would have begun the program 16 months sooner. A "no" would have allowed the engineer to move on to another project, or ask for a higher review, rather than waste his time battling the buck-passers.

A "play-it-safe" philosophy can be contagious, and can eat away at the will of even our most dedicated people. This company was built by people willing to take thoughtful but decisive action at every level. Let's keep it that way. Take a broad view of your responsibilities. Take some risks. The success of our business depends on your willingness to be daring and innovative.

T. Vincent Learson

I am concerned about the amount of confidential internal information that seems to be getting outside the business. For example, weeks before System/370 was publicly announced, the press was publishing accounts of what it was and what it would do. Days before we announced our fixed-term lease plan we were receiving calls asking for "confirmation" or "additional information."

How does such information get out in advance? So far as I can tell after some checking, most of it wasn't stolen or bought. Most of it was given away, by IBMers.

They did it in bits and pieces, unwittingly. In most cases, I suspect, they did it during casual conversations at social gatherings with friends or acquaintances. But the effect, in the long run, is just as harmful as if someone deliberately ransacked our files.

A great many very interested people watch the data processing industry, and, for obvious reasons, watch IBM in particular. They may be trade press reporters, stock traders, or, most important, competitors. But they are experts. They don't need many clues to draw some very accurate, meaningful conclusions.

The people who hear things from us can be above suspicion. But, they will speak to others. And this goes on – and is supported and amplified by other information – until a whole picture emerges, always at the wrong time and place.

One of the problems is that, in the course of our work, we communicate freely – sometimes too freely. We hear things we don't really need to know. We tell others things they don't really need to know. Information exchanged so casually comes to be regarded as common knowledge. The computer we're testing, and who it's being made for – a marketing strategy – a policy change – a new vendor contract – a technology advance – things that are routine on the job take on a completely different value in the hands of outsiders.

The solution to this problem, which I think accounts for the major share of our security "leaks," is obvious and rests largely in your hands. As managers, you must establish security-awareness as a key element in the general atmosphere of your departments. Your people must come to regard need-to-know as a way of life. It can't be done in one day. But I'm relying on you, by your example and follow-through, to keep emphasizing security until the leaks are plugged.

It's not just a matter of protecting business property. It's a question of what's right and what's wrong. I believe that it should be a matter of personal honor with every one of us in IBM not to divulge company information to anyone except those who have a need to know.

T. Vincent Learson

Number 6-71: December 10, 1971

It has long been our practice to encourage IBMers to become involved in their schools, governments, charities, and community agencies. And I'm pleased that so many contribute their time and effort to these activities either as volunteers or as elected or appointed officials.

This kind of community service, however, can lead an unwary person into a real or potential conflict of interest situation that could leave both the individual and the company open to public criticism. The best safeguard for every IBMer serving in such a capacity is simply this: whenever the group is considering a proposal from which IBM might benefit – or might appear to benefit – excuse yourself from the discussion and definitely abstain from voting.

In recognizing this need for sensitivity, however, I hope no IBM employee will be deterred from entering community affairs because of fear of criticism. There are bound to be times when partisans to one cause or another will see things that simply are not there and will try to make capital of them. This is one of the risks of public life that those people in it learn to absorb.

The IBMers serving in their communities today have my congratulations and thanks. What they are doing helps their communities, themselves and IBM.

T. Vincent Learson

Number 1-72: January 18, 1972

Once again, I'm writing you a *Management Briefing* on the subject of bureaucracy. Evidently the earlier ones haven't worked. So this time I'm taking a further step: I'm going directly to the individual employees in the company. You will be reading this poster and my comment on it in the forthcoming issue of *Think* magazine. But I wanted each one of you to have an advance copy because rooting out bureaucracy rests principally with the way each of us runs his own shop.

We've got to make a dent in this problem. By the time the *Think* piece comes out, I want the correction process already to have begun. And that job starts with you and with me.

Reprinted from *Think*, Volume 38, Number 1, 1972

'I'm Going to Do All I Can to Fight This Problem...'

A few weeks ago this poster arrived in the mail from a "group of concerned employees." They didn't sign it, apparently because they didn't know what I'd think of it.

I wish they *had* signed it because that's the way I like to receive mail, and because I'd like to have told them personally just this: I think it's exactly on target. I agree with it completely.

When I suggested we publish it, one general manager said, "Not unless you announce some new action to go with it."

Well, we've done just that. You will find at the beginning of this issue details about our recent organization changes.

Months ago I sent out a *Management Briefing* to condemn a principal feature of bureaucracy – the tendency of some people in IBM to pass the buck, play it safe, run from risks. But today we have still too many organizational procedures, still too many safeguards to keep people out of trouble, still too much refusal to delegate, still too much group thinking – the kind that almost never produces brilliant insight or decisive action.

Some signs are in the wind that many of you are beginning to rebel against excessive administration. This poster is one such sign. Another is a series of complaints I've been getting from IBMers giving examples of what they call "spinning our wheels": the army of sign-offs needed to approve a new product; the multiplication of task forces – proof that the assigned team has broken down; internal competition that ceases to be productive; minor non-concurrences, just for the record, which escalate simple decisions.

One of our top facility managers recently told me that no subject of any consequence could come up in his location without somebody's calling a meeting and having 30 people show up. His observation in itself proves his inability to correct this problem. Another IBMer wrote to me, almost in despair, of his concern – middle management has no conviction – and ended his letter, "Mr. Learson, maybe our company is too big to be productive. I sometimes yearn for the days when we were innovative and responsive to customer needs."

I'm seriously disturbed by the signs of bureaucracy, especially in times like these. And I'm delighted that people

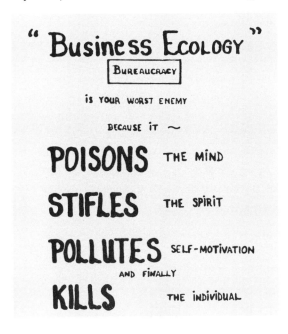

"Business Ecology"

Bureaucracy

is your worst enemy

because it ~

POISONS THE MIND

STIFLES THE SPIRIT

POLLUTES SELF-MOTIVATION

AND FINALLY

KILLS THE INDIVIDUAL

are calling a halt. Here's an assurance I want to give you: In this new year, I'm going to do all I can to fight this problem in these ways:

- Through taking a continuing hard look at the company's organization, in light of this problem, to see how we can tighten up;
- Through getting people at the top of the business to focus more on long-term goals, less on day-to-day monitoring;
- Through encouraging people to take on accountability for a job, leaving to them the details of how they do it;
- Through pushing decisions down the ladder where they belong, giving more IBMers a chance to exercise responsibility.

On all these projects I want your help.

- Question every procedure: if it doesn't make sense, break your back to replace it with one that does;
- Lean into the wind: don't take yesterday's prescription as an answer tomorrow;
- Don't go by the rule book and use the system as an excuse for senseless action or no action at all;
- Finally, move the ball forward by doing the little things: picking up the phone, making a quick call and getting the job done yourself; getting out of your office chair and walking to where the answer is; following through on something without bringing in an international conference to help you; scribbling a note instead of having it typed with 20 copies; trying to keep your organization small and your responsibilities increasing.

If you are a manager, I expect you to *find, recognize, and reward* people with this kind of style. No employee should ever again have to write me on this subject. If all of us get as hot under the collar as the IBMers who sent me this poster, maybe we can start to turn this whole bureaucracy thing around.

T. Vincent Learson

Number 2-72: February 4, 1972

I've long been convinced we have great depth and quality in our managerial ranks and that, given the opportunity, you are capable of making outstanding business decisions. A good example came up recently, and I wanted to share it with you.

As you know, we are taking a hard look these days at many IBM programs, to be sure they are still of value to the company. As an example, I recently asked if IBM is really benefiting from our annual $2.5 million expenditure for the Tuition Refund Plan.

The answer was an unqualified "yes," and here is why. When we established the Tuition Refund Plan 12 years ago, we gave it a clear-cut purpose and then put complete decision-making responsibility with each employee's immediate manager, the person in the best position to relate the Plan to the needs and potential of his people. Controls were minimized and second-guessing by higher levels of management was eliminated.

Since then thousands of managers, in individual decisions, have determined how we spend our Tuition Refund money. You have spent it wisely, and I am convinced that the high quality of your decisions is a tribute both to your good judgment and to the non-bureaucratic nature of the program.

I want to encourage this kind of management practice everywhere in the business. Once an objective has been set, the authority to make it happen should be delegated to the level of the business at which the facts are available and where effective, timely action can be taken. Our first-line managers are the backbone of IBM. I want to be sure we take every advantage of their skills and experience.

Frank T. Cary

Briefings 1-73 through 3-80
1973 – 1980

Frank T. Cary

Number 1-73: March 26, 1973

I can't remember a time when the ranks of IBM management needed greater resiliency, imagination and enthusiasm than at this point in our history. We all know why. The marketplace is changing constantly. We are working our way through a revolution in technology. In the face of changed manpower requirements, there is the difficult challenge of keeping employee morale and motivation at a high level.

In that environment, it's clear that we as managers have to keep the lines of communication with our people wide open, must willingly accept responsibility, take reasonable risks – do all the things we've urged upon, and demanded of IBM managers in times past.

Yet I'm not sure we're doing this task as well as we're able. In one recent Open Door case, for example, a good employee's advancement was blocked because he'd made one mistake – and his management didn't want to risk his repeating the mistake. That didn't make much sense, in my judgment. Soundly managed risk is what IBM is all about, and if that's what we want, we can't penalize a good employee indefinitely for a single mistake.

Another way to abdicate the management responsibility is to pass the buck – blame someone higher up for a difficult or unpopular decision. This "transparent" manager explains such a decision to his people in terms of "they" – it's their responsibility, not his or hers. To managers resting comfortably in that stance, I commend the old adage: "Fight up, support down." It's as useful a guideline as it ever was.

The fundamentals of good management, in my opinion, are enduring. But theory is one thing, practice quite another. Effective management demands continual refreshment, continual rededication, continual personal resolve. That is what I am asking of you – a personal resolve to reach this year toward a new level of management vitality.

Frank T. Cary

Number 2-73: April 23, 1973

Recently I learned that some IBMers had engaged in short sales of the securities of some competitors. This type of activity can cast doubt not only on the integrity of the individual but also on the reputation of IBM.

Accordingly, I want to make very clear that there are two types of investments which all IBMers and members of their immediate families should avoid:

– The "conflict of interest" investment in the stock of a competitor or supplier – a transaction that might interfere, or even appear to interfere, with the independent exercise of judgment in the best interest of IBM.

– The "inside" transaction – any buying or selling which is based, even in part, on information obtained on the job and which is not available to all investors.

Further, for many of us, *any* dealing in the stocks of competitors or suppliers should be avoided. Those whose professional or managerial responsibility involves working with information about a competitor or supplier should refrain from buying and selling such stocks. This point will be covered in a revision of the *Business Conduct Guidelines* that will be sent to your location shortly.

I recognize that the ultimate responsibility for avoiding questionable business transactions must lie with the individual. Your role as managers is to insure that your people understand our policy. If you are unable to answer a question about the propriety of a specific investment, you should consult with your manager or IBM legal counsel.

Frank T. Cary

Number 3-73: July 17, 1973

I am frequently asked what key qualities I look for in a manager. Certainly one of them is a sensitivity in dealing with and helping the people with whom he or she works. IBM managers have always had a reputation for their concern about people, but it's not often that we get any insight into what that means, and its value to IBM. A few letters I received recently provide such insight.

One came from the widow of an IBMer who died recently. She wrote to say how much help her husband's manager had been in her bereavement, handling many details for her and building her confidence in the future. In another letter, an IBMer wanted me to know how patient and considerate his manager had been in helping him overcome a long period of depression. An IBMer in upstate New York wrote to tell me that many people in his branch office, with management's support, had pitched in to help save his lakefront home from rising flood waters. Another IBMer waited until he transferred to a new area and a new manager to tell me how much he appreciated the genuine concern his former manager had demonstrated for him in all their dealings together.

It is not easy for a manager to know when he or she should go that extra step in demonstrating concern for the individual. While on the one hand IBMers have come to expect management to care about them, they also expect management to respect their privacy and not meddle in their personal business.

I can give you no firm guidelines for negotiating this tightrope. It demands, situation by situation, the careful exercise of management judgment. The letters I receive demonstrate there is much you can do and are doing to keep alive IBM's tradition of concern for the individual, in action as well as words. It's vital that we each resolve to help sustain and build upon that tradition.

Frank T. Cary

Number 4-73: August 3, 1973

One of IBM's hard-earned advantages is our lead time on new products – and we put a lot of research and development effort into securing it. But if there is a security leak, that lead time advantage can be lost very quickly and, with it, the money and effort we have invested, and the ingenuity of our people.

All this became painfully clear recently when a group of people in California was arrested and charged with offenses related to the theft of IBM trade secrets. The following letter, commenting on that situation and its meaning, is scheduled to appear in the August issue of *Think*, and I send it to you in advance so you may think about this matter and focus on it with your people.

We must all face up to the implications of a security breach. When a leak occurs, the press begins speculating about product announcements; the customer is confused; the competition has a chance to rush a rival product to market very profitably; and our long-term planning is jeopardized.

Such exposures have occurred more than once, at great cost. Management attitude is the answer – not more security guards. The best controls will be inadequate if you, as managers, don't take the security problem seriously enough. Penalties must be clearly understood – and firmly implemented. I do not want to see the vital flow of information within the company inhibited by bureaucratic controls – but I do want each of you to talk this subject through with your people, and lead by example.

Chairman's Letter
Think, Volume 39, Number 6, 1973

Fellow IBMers:

I'm sure most of you were shocked to read in the press that a group of people was arrested and charged with offenses related to the theft of IBM trade secrets. It's particularly sobering that all this took place despite our increased security precautions during the past several years.

Every business, if it is to survive, has to have some safeguards, some protection of its proprietary assets. In IBM, as our use of technology becomes broader and broader, embracing such diverse disciplines as electronics, physics and chemistry, we have far less ability to protect what we are doing and the products we are making. It is therefore more important than ever to secure the know-how we already have. This know-how represents hundreds of millions of dollars – not only in development work done, but also in potential revenue from the products this work makes possible.

Now in protecting proprietary information, we don't want to generate mistrust of one another, or turn the company into a fortress, or let the actions of a few diminish our dedication to high standards of performance and creativity. These would be extremes we could not accept.

But we don't want to be naive either. However much we dislike it, however much we would all prefer an open environment in which to work, we must ask people to wear badges, put special locks on doors, and require documents to be signed out formally. It is a bother and a nuisance, but it is absolutely necessary.

Despite these steps, we cannot safeguard the essentials of our business unless each of us makes security his or her personal responsibility. I ask your continuing understanding, and vigil.

Frank T. Cary

Frank T. Cary

Number 5-73: August 31, 1973

In many walks of life today, we are seeing a conflict between the willingness of people to stand up for their own convictions and their desire to be considered loyal members of the team.

Fighting for your convictions can be a lonely business. But it's my observation that the people who get ahead in IBM are the ones who are willing to do just that. This course is not without its hazards. To be thoughtful, sure of your facts, and firm in stating your point of view, however, is the very essence of good, courageous management.

By contrast, to accept without challenge the opinions of others when you believe them to be wrong is to let down the team. There is a name for this type of conformity – "groupthink." We have all met people who voice business judgments in private that they would never express officially for fear of incurring disfavor. Others have been known to tailor reports or proposals to reflect what they think their management wants to hear.

This aim-to-please philosophy can have serious consequences for IBM. If we avoid raising valid objections, or suggesting new alternatives, or questioning weak premises, we run the risk of undermining our decision-making processes.

We need managers who are willing to challenge the conventional wisdom when their convictions and the facts demand it. That's the sort of courageous management I'm looking for in IBM.

Frank T. Cary

Number 6-73: October 10, 1973

Recently, an employee with many years of IBM service was forced to resign because a request for a transfer from one city to another was denied – a request made because of a pressing personal commitment. Management at both the transferring and receiving locations had made all the appropriate inquiries and had found no suitable openings.

They gave up too quickly.

No one worked hard enough to identify jobs likely to open up in the near future. No one looked at job possibilities other than the one the IBM employee was holding – jobs which could have been learned relatively quickly. No one gave enough weight to the fact that the employee had performed well for many years in IBM, and didn't want to leave. In short, no one – not even the employee's manager, made an extra effort. Within a month, as it turned out, several suitable openings developed. Aware of this and understandably bitter, the employee wrote to tell me so, and has since been reinstated.

"The system" in this case obviously failed. But systems are created by people, and people can improve them. I do not suggest that we throw out our rule books or ignore our traditional personnel practices in dealing with our people. But it's helpful to remember that IBM's guidelines for managers generally represent the minimum we are required to do. The managers who impress me the most are those who view guidelines as the starting point, not the finish line.

We take great pride in our concern for the individual in IBM. Let's act on that conviction.

Frank T. Cary

Number 7-73: November 30, 1973

Now that we have Judge Christensen's final ruling in the Telex-IBM case, we will file our appeal against the basic anti-trust decision of the court. We have several reasons to believe our appeal has substantial merit. Among those reasons is Judge Christensen's own statement that the case involves a "controlling question of law as to which there is substantial ground for differences of opinion...."

Although we will do everything possible to expedite our appeal, the process will probably take some time. I think you should know, as managers, how the decision affects our business in the meantime.

As you know, we have agreed with Telex that neither party will attempt to collect damages until a final judgment is reached. Also, the injunctive relief to Telex – the steps we must take in the way we conduct our business – has been revised considerably from the directives of the September 17 ruling.

For example, the original ruling would have required us to release electronic interface information on new IBM products at the time of our announcement of such products, or when our development labs turned over such products to our manufacturing facilities. The amended ruling directs us to make available on request such information at the time of our first customer shipment, which is consistent with our past and current practice.

The amended ruling also clarifies our responsibility in the area of "add-on" memory. The original judgment seemed to indicate we would have to price separately all computer memories, even those that are an integral part of the central processing unit. The new ruling directs us to price separately only those memory devices "which are not a single product with the central processing unit." That is essentially what we have been doing.

We also are enjoined under the amended ruling, for a period of three years, from collecting termination charges or liquidated damages because of cancellation of any long-term lease agreement on our peripheral products. As you may know, we suspended the collection of such charges on September 18, pending the final outcome of the case so, in effect, the court's injunctions require us to continue day-to-day business practices in substantially the same way as we do at present.

Yet we still feel strongly that the ruling is erroneous in its interpretations of antitrust law and in its reading of the intent of certain IBM business decisions. For example, in his amended findings the judge said "there was no evidence that IBM reduced prices below cost and a reasonable profit." Yet he still found the price reductions "predatory." A price yielding a reasonable profit has always been lawful, and we reject the judge's view of IBM's pricing actions. We will appeal this issue among others as we move forward with our appeal.

Although it is somewhat encouraging to all of us that the court has reduced the damages awarded to Telex by $93 million and has substantially modified the injunctive relief, we still believe the basic ruling against IBM is wrong, and I'm confident we can demonstrate that IBM has competed fairly and within the law.

Frank T. Cary

Number 1-74: February 26, 1974

I'm sure you're all aware of IBM's commitment to Affirmative Action in providing equal opportunity for minorities and women.

We've made good progress on one of our objectives – bringing into IBM capable and highly motivated minorities and women.

Our second objective is taking longer to achieve: helping minorities and women qualify themselves for advancement at every level of the business consistent with their abilities and their growing population in the company.

The relevant question I'm asked most frequently by IBM managers is: "How can we do that without practicing reverse discrimination?"

My answer is that we will not compromise our policy of promoting the most competent, most qualified people. But what we all have to do as managers is provide whatever extra help and learning opportunities may be needed to shorten the time necessary for minorities and women to compete on an equal footing with other IBMers. The best individuals will still be selected for promotion, but we intend to make the competition keener.

We have tripled the number of minorities and women in the ranks of management over the past five years. That's not a bad start, but I'm convinced we can do better.

Frank T. Cary

Number 2-74: March 14, 1974

One important conclusion that I draw from our employee opinion surveys is that morale relates less to the ups and downs of the business and more to sound management accomplished through frank and open communication.

Our business has to undergo changes constantly. It's vital that these changes should not seem mysterious or unreasonable to the people affected by them. Our responsibility as managers is to make the reason clear, whether it's a change of mission or method, a reorganization, a merging of functions, or an attempt to address some new business opportunity. The message may be negative – the discontinuance of a mission or consolidation of staffs, for example – but it is essential that there be a common understanding of why we do what we do.

From time to time, we as managers should all ask ourselves some hard questions about how well we communicate. Have we made good use of personal discussions and group meetings to increase communication – *two*-way communication – with our people? Have we spelled out our objectives for the months ahead? Have we been candid about business problems? Have we explained why changes are necessary? And if you as managers don't have answers to give, I would urge you to ask questions yourselves.

The words of one employee – "I'll do or die, but tell me why" – may seem extreme, but they help me make my point. IBMers have demonstrated a remarkable adaptability to change. We owe them all the information and understanding we can provide.

Frank T. Cary

Number 3-74: May 20, 1974

Since we have been hiring again in significant numbers, there has been an increase in complaints against us by unsuccessful job applicants. Last year, 16 people filed charges with government agencies, alleging discriminatory hiring practices by IBM. In the first quarter of this year alone, there were five such complaints.

These may seem like small numbers, considering the thousands of people we interview each year, but they reflect a real problem, and we must address it. Today's applicants tend to be more assertive than in the 1960s. They ask more penetrating questions about the company and its policies. If they are not hired, they want to know why. And if the answers we give them seem unconvincing, they do not hesitate to complain – sometimes without foundation.

It is healthy that the opportunity for redress of real grievances exists, but I would like to think that for applicants to IBM, it is unnecessary. Unsuccessful candidates should always go away with the feeling that they have been fairly and courteously treated.

A hiring decision should be made only after careful evaluation of the candidate. A decision not to hire should be conveyed clearly and respectfully – and it should be communicated to the applicant without delay.

If you are in doubt as to how to deal with job applicants, ask yourself what you would wish if you were on the other side of the desk – what you would consider straightforward, courteous treatment. Then act accordingly.

In today's employment environment, we must be prepared to go the extra mile and use all our management skill to be fair-minded and considerate to applicants – not just because the government requires it, but because it is right.

Frank T. Cary

Number 4-74: July 11, 1974

One of our executives recently learned that a member of an employee's family urgently needed specialized medical attention, available only at a hospital a great distance from home. The family couldn't afford the cost of the trip and the situation was not covered by our benefit plans.

In such situations, I want to be sure we respond in a helpful way, if we can – and that we don't turn aside just because the answer is not specified in the *Manager's Manual*. In this particular case, with a little extra effort, an appropriate way was found to give special assistance and the situation was greatly eased.

The emergencies that qualify for such help are hard to define, but the philosophy with which we should approach them is clear: to keep alive in IBM that special sense of concern for the individual – what we sometimes think of as the "small company attitude."

We cannot provide for all circumstances, and there will be some distressing situations in which IBM cannot get involved. But I do want you to be alert to cases of unusual hardship and to review them with your own management if you feel there is a role for the company to play. Your initiative, sound instinct and good judgment can make a large difference at such critical times.

Frank T. Cary

Number 5-74: November 20, 1974

For both business and family reasons, we as managers should be sensitive to the problems that our people may face when they accept new assignments involving physical moves. We all know that moves can be disruptive for families and that the rising prices of homes and mortgages may compound the problem.

Before offering a job to someone from another area, therefore, I think we should ask ourselves: "Is this move really necessary?" Often there are options, and it is entirely reasonable to attempt to fill openings locally.

There are times when a move is essential – for instance, when a certain skill is urgently needed or when organization or workload changes make a move necessary. When we determine that a relocation is necessary, we should be sure the employee fully understands what is involved in relocation and has an opportunity to investigate the costs, the housing situation, and the new surroundings.

We will always need people who are willing to take on challenges anywhere, anytime. They are a great asset to the company, and their moves may be vital to the business as well as to their personal career development. But moving is not the only way up the ladder, and the costs can outweigh the benefits. Sensitivity and good business judgment indicate that managers should carefully weigh the alternatives.

Frank T. Cary

Number 6-74: December 12, 1974

Recently, I learned of several instances in which managers have misused the appraisal system. In each case, the manager had lowered an employee's appraisal rating as a punitive measure because of a lone incident – an instance of insensitivity, or an isolated mistake.

This is the wrong way to use the appraisal program. Its purpose is to review and evaluate the employee's performance over a period of time – typically a year – and to counsel him or her on ways to be more effective. Certainly, the appraisal will reflect the ups and downs of day-to-day performance, but an appraisal rating should not be reduced – or raised, for that matter – on the basis of a single incident.

There are exceptions, of course. If an employee's performance has been deteriorating, one more incident may represent the culmination of a series of problems. Similarly, an event may bring to light a history of deficiencies and shortcomings the manager had not suspected. A reduced appraisal rating may then be justified, provided the manager makes clear to the employee that the decision is based on long-standing performance deficiencies.

By and large, however, managers should be able to deal with isolated mistakes or lapses of judgment through counseling. It is essential to the integrity of the appraisal system that appraisals reflect overall performance and not just isolated performance in a single incident.

Frank T. Cary

Number 1-75: January 27, 1975

Our Open Door policy has been an important and effective way of addressing IBMers' problems for many years, so I am concerned to hear reports which indicate that some IBMers do not understand it. Specifically, there have been occasions recently when IBMers have found it necessary to go outside the company to tackle problems which could well have been solved through the Open Door – if the employee had known enough about it and been willing to trust it.

My faith in the program is firm because I know from personal experience the large amount of management time that is devoted to the investigation and resolution of Open Door cases. I am convinced that the Open Door is one of our foremost assurances that respect for the individual is much more than just a slogan in IBM.

To keep the program working, however, we need managers who will demonstrate their faith in the Open Door, and in themselves, by making sure employees understand what it is and how it works. The best time to do that is *before* problems arise so that a level of mutual trust in the policy is well established.

It is a key management responsibility to be certain employees know about the procedures for assuring fair treatment in IBM and to make it clear that we take our responsibilities in this area very seriously.

Frank T. Cary

Number 2-75: May 22, 1975

The number of employees participating in IBM's Suggestion Plan has fallen by more than half since 1970. This decline would be regrettable at any time. In today's inflationary environment, it is a cause for serious concern. For the best weapon we have against inflation is increased productivity, and one of the keys to greater productivity is the Suggestion Plan. Over the years, it has been the vehicle for putting thousands of cost-saving, labor-saving ideas to work.

To counter the present decline, we have set in motion a program to revitalize the Plan by providing more thorough evaluation of suggestions and shortening the turnaround time involved. The success of the program depends directly on the support of all IBM managers. The best suggestion in the world can come to nothing if it encounters management indifference.

I want each of you to do your part. First, make a personal commitment to encourage employees to participate in the Suggestion Plan. Second, help them develop and submit good ideas. Third, if you are asked to evaluate a suggestion, remember that you have an obligation to be conscientious and to give the matter priority attention. Finally, if an idea is adopted, make sure the employee receives proper recognition for it. If it isn't adopted, it's equally important to give the reasons promptly and in a frank but encouraging manner.

Encouraging employees' ideas and treating them with respect will demonstrate in the most positive way that we need the imagination of all of our people to help move the business ahead – now more than ever.

Frank T. Cary

Number 3-75: June 20, 1975

A recent Open Door case concerns an IBMer whose personal problems had been so widely discussed by his management that, some three years after they were worked out, his reputation was still adversely affected.

Fortunately, this is not a common situation. But it does illustrate what can happen when we fail to protect an individual's right to privacy.

IBM has taken a number of steps to preserve the privacy of its people. We have removed unnecessary information from the forms we use routinely in the business. We have established guidelines to limit the access to and govern the retention of files and records.

But these steps cannot prevent the injury to individuals that can result from loose talk. Managing in IBM almost always involves being entrusted with confidential information about other IBMers. Gossip has no place in good management and for managers to forget that is worse than a failure of judgment; it is a breach of trust.

We can, and should, look into our handling of files and the information in them from a privacy viewpoint – but this is only half the job. Privacy preserved by common sense and mutual respect is equally indispensable. That has been our long-standing policy in IBM, and it is up to managers to put the policy into practice.

Frank T. Cary

Number 4-75: August 4, 1975

We recently completed the best revenue-producing first six months in the history of the company, an outstanding feat that merits congratulations and thanks. But, paradoxically, our year-to-date results are also a cause for concern.

For while gross income from operations increased nearly $507 million, up 8 percent over the comparable period for last year, costs jumped nearly $576 million, up by 12 percent, and, as you know, net profit actually fell.

What this means is that all the hard work and resourcefulness that go into developing and manufacturing our products and increasing sales volumes can be totally offset unless we do a better job of managing costs. For the real measure of success is not revenue alone, but revenue in relation to costs. While not every manager has a marketing responsibility, every manager does have a responsibility to ensure that IBM costs don't outpace our income.

Many of you have already helped the corporation take positive actions to bring our resources into balance:

- We have shifted work from one IBM location to another. Almost every plant throughout the world has been involved in workload transfers of this kind.
- Over 2,000 volunteers worldwide have been accepted for transfer to other locations, moving to where the work is. Many people have received extensive retraining – a quarter of them for entirely new careers.
- As part of the special opportunity program in the U.S., nearly 2,000 IBMers with long service have left the company voluntarily under special financial arrangements.

I continue to be impressed by the flexibility of our people in responding to the needs of the business. And while there are some indications that the recession is bottoming out, we cannot afford to let up in our efforts.

As we continue our efforts to increase sales volumes, we must simultaneously take every measure to trim expense. That is the key to productivity and future growth, and every IBMer can take part in achieving it.

We are faced with a need for productivity awareness at every level in every area of the business. That's our responsibility as managers. I would like each of you to communicate your own cost control messages by every means at your disposal to make cost consciousness and productivity an ingrained way of doing business.

Frank T. Cary

Number 5-75: September 19, 1975

During 1975, some 1600 IBMers in the U.S. will become managers for the first time. For many, the experience will bring distinctly mixed emotions – the sense of achievement that comes with new responsibility and some uneasiness about their ability to handle it successfully. Even for the most self-reliant people, the transition to management can be difficult.

I'm frequently asked if I have any words of advice for new managers. My first impulse is to say no. Over the years, I've grown very skeptical of formulas for "how to be a successful manager." People are different, jobs are different, and there are lots of different management styles that work. But if there is one piece of advice that I can offer, it is this: *Be yourself.* Don't try to imitate anyone else. All of us, of course, pick up useful techniques by observing other people – their ways of handling work, planning time, or delegating responsibility. But to do things exactly the way somebody else does them, to take on someone else's style or personality, is to run the risk of seeming insincere.

New managers sometimes ask if there is such a thing as an IBM management style. I suppose that to the extent we favor any style at all, it is an *active* style. By this I mean that we want managers who do more than just provide goals for their people and then wait for them to succeed or fail. The best managers become actively involved with their people and what they are trying to accomplish.

By and large, new managers will evolve their own individual approaches. This is as it should be. So long as they bring out the energies and talents of their people, they will be managing in the best tradition of IBM – regardless of style.

Frank T. Cary

Number 6-75: December 22, 1975

In a recent Speak Up, an employee wrote: "I want to express my sincere appreciation to IBM for all the courtesies and kindnesses extended to me on the occasion of my retirement. I was made to feel really important.... The company demonstrated once again that it has a genuine concern for its people."

Such comments show that the special attention we pay to our personal relationships with employees is appreciated – whether it's a luncheon for a retiree, a silver spoon for a new-born child, or an expression of condolence.

By and large, IBM managers are effective in encouraging our people in their work and recognizing them for their achievements. But when it comes to special forms of personal recognition, there is considerable evidence that some managers are not sufficiently sensitive and responsive.

This concerns me because good human relations are the responsibility of management. Programs designed to help us in this area can succeed only to the extent that they are fully utilized by managers and carried out with true warmth and concern. Ignored, or performed perfunctorily, they not only fail in their purpose but create the opposite impression – that the company has lost touch with the individual or has substituted mechanical procedures.

I realize that you have a lot to concentrate on these days to keep our business strong in a tough economic environment. But good human relations lie at the very heart of our business. As the company continues to grow and change, it becomes more important than ever to remember that personal recognition is vital to everyone.

The immediate manager is in the best position to know of major events in an employee's life – a birth, death or illness in the family, a service anniversary, retirement – and to respond to them in a sensitive, personal and meaningful way.

Frank T. Cary

Number 1-76: April 5, 1976

For over 16 years, the IBM Speak Up program has served as a special two-way communications channel through which IBM people can ask questions or tell management when they feel something is going wrong.

Still working, and still a cornerstone of IBM employee relations, Speak Up is nonetheless beginning to show some signs of erosion. There has been a slow decline in employee use of the program – down a third since 1969 – and a slow increase in the number of unsigned Speak Ups. I am writing to you to enlist your help in reversing these trends.

It's clear to me that most managers make a sincere attempt to provide straightforward answers to Speak Ups. You devote considerable time investigating employee concerns. That's as it should be, because every Speak Up deserves our full attention.

But, occasionally, management answers have been viewed as "canned," "evasive," or "a list of excuses that didn't bring any action." Some employees have doubts about the anonymity of the program. They fear their managers might regard them as troublemakers if they voice criticism. Equally disturbing, some managers worry that the program might reflect badly on them.

Speak Up should be seen in a more positive and realistic light: a special program to give employees a way to question or comment about anything in IBM and get an answer – with absolutely no fear of retribution.

In general, we should not offer interviews to employees who didn't ask for them in their Speak Ups. This could lead to suspicions about our motives and might compromise the integrity of the program.

You have helped build Speak Ups into an outstanding program. It has brought credit to IBM because we put a confidential system in place that asks for employee questions and comments, and we have done our best to face up to them. Let's keep it that way.

Frank T. Cary

Number 2-76: August 6, 1976

Our resource management controls, in place now for more than 18 months, have been remarkably effective. They have helped us preserve full employment, achieve an overall reduction in our work force, keep control of costs, and increase our productivity. Most of the time, the controls work. I want to talk about the times when they don't.

At a recent lab directors meeting, I heard about a manager who needed a programmer. He decided to transfer someone from a distant location from within his own division. An equally qualified programmer was available just down the hall but from another division. Rather than try for an exception to division constraints by transferring the local person, the manager tried to bring in the person from the distant location. He was more concerned about the division's objectives than the objectives of IBM as a whole.

In times of resource constraint, we have to have rules; but rules should never be substituted for good sense. When a rule does not make sense for our employees and our business, that rule should be appealed. In this case, the manager should have requested an exception from the division.

In the overwhelming majority of instances, managers in IBM have done a superb job with resource management problems, and it has been a difficult task.

Resource management is going to be with us for the foreseeable future. Its purpose is to utilize available skills and further increase productivity. There will always be a need for certain rules and controls, but when those rules conflict with what you think is right, I expect every manager to speak out and make exceptions.

Frank T. Cary

Number 3-76: August 27, 1976

"It's not my problem" is an attitude we can't tolerate in IBM. I expect all managers to enforce corporate policy not only in their own areas of responsibility but in any area when circumstances demand it. Two recent incidents show what I mean.

At a Family Dinner, some employees ignored company policy by bringing alcoholic drinks into the room where the dinner was being held. Several managers saw what was happening, but either did nothing about it or failed to take effective action to stop it.

During a branch office presentation, an employee from another division used profane and vulgar language. There were several managers in the audience, but all were hesitant to interrupt the presentation because the speaker was not from their own division.

Unquestionably, specific responsibility in such situations rests with the host manager, who should ensure that these kinds of things don't happen. Nevertheless, if, despite careful planning, an incident does occur, then it is the responsibility of any manager present to take action to resolve the problem. In the cases I've mentioned, the managers who witnessed the incidents – and who later explained that, for one reason or another, they did not intervene – were seriously at fault.

When it is clear that *any* company policy is being disregarded, *any* manager who is present and aware of the situation should assume IBM management responsibility and take immediate action.

Frank T. Cary

Number 4-76: September 17, 1976

In recent Speak Ups, a significant number of people have complained about the environment in which they work. To quote from just one: "While I understand that effective cost controls can and should be implemented by any business, I feel there are certain areas which should not be cut. Cleanliness of one's working environment is one of those areas." Other Speak Ups describe such unsatisfactory conditions as unswept floors, unwashed windows, littered grounds, safety and health hazards.

Such complaints are a matter of great concern to me, especially when they are linked by the writers to our cost control efforts. A safe, clean and healthful working environment has always been a hallmark of IBM. It should be a matter of pride to every manager. While we are all trying hard to keep costs down, we must also maintain IBM as a high quality place to work.

The Speak Ups reveal very plainly that people associate the condition of their working environment with the company's concern and respect for the individual. Reasonable financial controls are one thing. Bad housekeeping is another. Let's cut costs, not corners.

Frank T. Cary

Number 5-76: December 20, 1976

In IBM, we take pride in extending special help to any of our people who face a personal emergency: an accident, critical illness or family tragedy.

Our managers have a fine record of stepping up to these situations. Sometimes, however, circumstances make it difficult for a manager to act effectively alone. In such cases, you should not hesitate to obtain assistance from other locations or higher management.

Here's a case in point. Last summer, the Big Thompson River swept over its banks, some 30 miles from Boulder, killing more than a hundred people and injuring and marooning hundreds more. Managers at our Boulder location checked to see if any local employees were involved. Simultaneously, concerned managers at other locations – some as far away as the Mid-Hudson Valley – contacted Boulder inquiring about IBMers or their families who were vacationing in the flooded area.

A team from IBM Boulder went directly to the scene to obtain from rescue authorities the names of victims and those missing. With the help of both divisional and corporate personnel, these names were then matched against our personnel records to determine if any IBMers were involved. Fortunately, none were. In addition, IBMers from Boulder worked with community groups to assist the rescue efforts.

While this was a highly unusual situation, I feel that it was very well handled and that it says a lot about the company's concern for the well-being of our people, on the job or off. As managers, let's continue to make the extra effort that can mean so much to our people when they need our help.

Frank T. Cary

Number 1-77: February 3, 1977

Recent publicity about IBM's attitude on the participation of employees in public service activities has led some people to think that there has been a fundamental change in our policy. That is not the case, and I would like every manager to have a clear understanding of what our policy is.

It is one of IBM's oldest traditions to encourage our people to involve themselves in political, public service, and social service activities – to be good citizens of their communities. Managers have done their best to accommodate employees who have asked for time off whenever that is appropriate and reasonable. Under the Fund for Community Service, the company has provided financial support for many useful community projects to which IBMers were personally committed.

At the same time, IBM has had to make every effort to avoid real or potential conflict of interest situations, especially where IBMers hold elective or appointive public office, or campaign for themselves or others for such posts. Over time, as employee requests for time off for a wide range of activities have increased, we have issued guidelines for dealing with them. Since interpretations by managers at different IBM locations have sometimes lacked consistency, we issued a revision of the *Manager's Manual* last October, which gave rise to the recent publicity.

While most community activity goes on after working hours, there are situations in which company time off is requested and in order. In the case of public office activity (e.g., where an IBMer is a legislator, mayor, school board member, etc., or campaigning for himself or others for such posts), IBM does not pay the employee for the company time taken but requires that it must be taken without pay, as vacation time, or made up where that can be arranged.

I hope that IBMers will continue to take an active part in civic and political life and that managers will continue to do their part in helping them do so, within the limits imposed by the need to avoid any conflict of interest – or the appearance of one – as a protection for both the individual and the company.

Frank T. Cary

Number 2-77: March 14, 1977

I recently learned of a distressing incident in which valuable company assets were being systematically stolen by employees. Although others were aware of what was happening, they did not report it.

Incidents of theft by employees are always a great disappointment to me, as I'm sure they are to you. We expect a lot more from IBM people. The act of stealing itself is abhorrent. Of equal concern, the failure of IBMers who witness such incidents to come forward to report them shows a lack of responsibility.

We have all heard or read about people who refuse to "get involved." This should not be the case in IBM.

As managers, you have a special obligation to maintain high standards of personal conduct and to communicate a positive security attitude to your people. It should be stressed that every IBMer has a personal responsibility to be involved in the protection of IBM assets. Anything stolen from our premises is stolen from all of us. Each individual suffers, not only from the theft but from the deterioration in work environment that results.

I expect all IBMers to protect company property as if it were their own.

Frank T. Cary

Number 3-77: April 7, 1977

For the first time, IBM's *Business Conduct Guidelines* is being distributed to all 291,000 IBM people throughout the world. Distribution of the English version is currently under way and the translated versions, in 15 major languages, will follow shortly.

I am writing to you to emphasize the importance I attach to the standards of conduct we expect every IBMer to follow. We have always put great reliance on the personal conduct of our people, and our confidence has been well placed.

We published the first edition of *Business Conduct Guidelines* in 1961 to make sure that IBMers understood the high ethical standards the company requires and how to apply them under actual business conditions. The *Guidelines* have been revised from time to time to keep them relevant. This latest revision is the most concise, direct statement of our ethical principles we have ever published, and I think our people will find it easy to read and understand.

I'm counting on every manager in IBM to give this book the time, thought and attention it deserves. I also want you to make sure that any questions your employees have about business conduct are fully answered. Later this year, many of our employees will be asked to certify – as in years past – that they have read the new *Guidelines*. Beyond that, it is my hope that every IBMer will read them.

Business conduct is not something that can be left to auditors and lawyers. It is the very cornerstone on which our business reputation is built, and it is one of our most prized assets. Ethical behavior starts with the individual; the principles that govern it must be a day-to-day way of life.

Frank T. Cary

Number 4-77: May 17, 1977

This year, for the first time since mid-1974, we are bringing new people into IBM in fairly sizeable numbers. I believe that selecting new employees is one of our most important responsibilities. We can achieve our employment goals only if each manager exercises this responsibility in a thoughtful and thorough manner.

Every manager should view the selection of new people as a major business decision. You should be completely familiar with the employment process, including ways to locate and evaluate outstanding men and women. A record of achievement, a high degree of initiative, and a willingness to adapt to change are essential qualities for any job in IBM.

Managers should prepare themselves to ask the right questions about the individual's qualifications and to answer questions about IBM policies and practices. In addition, you should be ready to discuss public issues that affect the company by keeping abreast of such topics in newspapers, magazines and company publications.

To remain an outstanding company demands outstanding people. Few managerial roles are as important to IBM's future as hiring the best qualified men and women we can find.

Frank T. Cary

Number 5-77: November 29, 1977

Recently, I met with a group of senior IBM executives to discuss fundamental strategies for the continued growth and success of the company. One that we all agreed on was the importance of managing our employees effectively.

While each of us might define the function of managing people somewhat differently, I personally think it means:

– telling employees exactly what's expected of them.
– compensating them on merit.
– helping them develop their full potential.
– providing reasonable performance plans and fair performance evaluations.
– giving constructive recommendations and criticism.

What this boils down to is helping people succeed in their jobs. Now that may sound simple, but it is basic to our success as a company. It is the key to meeting our business goals, improving our productivity and staying competitive.

IBM has been very fortunate to have excellent managers over the years. Many of us have benefited from working under such people, and I know every one of us, myself included, has fond memories of managers who helped us move ahead.

Just recently, I heard about a concerned manager who had a profound effect on the career of an employee. An assembly-line worker at a major IBM manufacturing location mentioned to her manager that her real ambition was to be a secretary. The manager helped her to enter the location's secretarial training program, and when she had completed it successfully, to get an assignment in personnel. She did so well that her new manager, believing she could do even more, arranged for her to transfer to OPD sales, where she has already made one Hundred Percent Club and seems well on her way to others.

The story is a reminder that being a good manager is more than just meeting deadlines, quotas and schedules and involves making the required effort to encourage and lead people. I know that all of you have been working very hard to keep the business operating successfully. I would urge you also to review the development needs of your employees regularly, and ask the question, "Is there something more I can do to help my people succeed in their jobs?"

Frank T. Cary

For over 50 years, the Suggestion Plan has helped keep IBM competitive by encouraging creative discontent – the urge to look for a better way. Employee suggestions have saved IBM $126.6 million in the United States over the last ten years alone, and more than a quarter of a million awards totaling $26.2 million have been presented for ingenuity and enterprise. That's an outstanding record, and I want to see it continue.

Unfortunately, over the last five years, the volume of suggestions has declined substantially. We recently announced changes in the plan that will make it more financially attractive. But money alone is not the answer. There are several things managers can do to improve participation.

A review of the program shows that one problem is long turnaround times. I'm sure each of us has handled a suggestion we could have moved along faster. Each suggestion – simple or complex, big savings or small – deserves our prompt attention.

Secondly, we ought to devote time to improving the quality of our evaluations. Sometimes, under the press of daily business, evaluations are done poorly. Another factor may be the attitude with which we approach a suggestion. The right way is to withhold judgment until we have carefully examined the merits of the idea. The wrong way is to say: "How can I knock this off?" – the "not invented here" syndrome. A good manager is always willing to adopt a change for the better, whether the suggester is within the department or outside it.

Further, once you or a member of your staff has evaluated a suggestion, ask yourself: "Is the response fair, understandable and courteous? Would I be satisfied to receive such an answer?"

As a manager, you can also help people initiate suggestions. Let your employees know that you're ready to discuss their ideas and to help put them on paper. Encourage them to be forces for change rather than custodians of the status quo. To help you do this, a videotape is now available from Personnel for use in department meetings. It explains the plan and tells the stories of three employees who won suggestion awards.

In its first 50 years, the Suggestion Plan has been good for IBM. Through the plan, our people have generated many cost-effective ideas that have helped our business grow. I am counting on you to insure its successful future.

Frank T. Cary

Number 1-79: February 28, 1979

A recent analysis of our performance planning, counseling and evaluation program shows that, although the program is sound in structure and philosophy, we must do a better job of carrying it out.

For example, according to the analysis, too many managers do not have performance plans; and too many employees and managers are not appraised on schedule.

These findings, in themselves, cause concern. But they are especially significant in light of another fact: One of the most important influences on managers' attitudes toward the program is the example set by their *own* managers. Thus, neglect on the part of managers at any level in supporting and implementing the program spreads to others.

Employee performance planning and evaluation is a fundamental part of the manager's job. I expect managers at *all* levels to prepare performance plans, to communicate with their people, and to appraise them regularly.

This is not a simple process, nor is it meant to be. The evaluation of employee performance is an ongoing effort. It takes time, perseverance and hard work. It is based on realistic performance plans, on revisions in those plans as needed, on counsel whenever either manager or employee thinks it desirable, and, finally, on fair and formal evaluations.

Our experience with the performance planning, counseling and evaluation program shows it is basic to building good communications and developing employee potential to the fullest. Both are key to our success as a company. I ask all managers at every level of the business to give the program their total support.

Frank T. Cary

Number 2-79: July 27, 1979

To cooperate with current national energy conservation efforts, IBM is undertaking several initiatives that need the support of managers if they are to be effective.

For example, we are encouraging our people to form carpools. Since pooling depends on groups of employees arriving at work and leaving at regular times, managers should take these arrangements into consideration in scheduling work assignments and meetings.

At facilities where staggered working hours are in effect to relieve traffic or other problems, managers should accommodate employees wishing to carpool by rearranging their work schedules, if possible.

IBM is also complying with federal regulations that call for buildings to be cooled no lower than 78 degrees in summer and heated no higher than 65 degrees in winter. For employees at many of our locations, the required temperatures should pose little or no hardship. But for others – particularly in the South and in the colder parts of the country – the reduced levels of air conditioning and heating could create some discomfort during part of the year.

I hope managers will make it a point to consider employee comfort in judging what is appropriate dress for their people in a particular work environment. This does *not* diminish IBM's traditional position on suitable business attire. It *does* suggest that managers should be flexible enough to make exceptions when common sense calls for them.

Let's remember that energy conservation requires the active cooperation of all of us if it is to be implemented with a minimum of inconvenience to our employees.

Frank T. Cary

Number 3-79: November 21, 1979

Over the past eight years, in measuring our progress toward meeting our equal opportunity goals, the government has audited IBM more than 600 times. Each time it has found us in compliance. That's good news, and we can be proud of our record. But I like to think that we had high standards for fair treatment before legal requirements ever were established, and that they continue to go beyond the requirements of the law.

That's why I'm troubled by a recent Open Door investigation that led to the discovery of a manager's serious errors in judgment about a minority employee's development and promotion.

The Open Door involved a minority employee who wanted to move into a job with greater responsibility – to be tested by more challenging work. His management's response was to ask the employee to prove over and over again that he was qualified to assume more responsibility. They wanted a "sure thing." They were reluctant to take a reasonable risk – the same kind of risk we all take each time we move someone into a more responsible job. Needless to say, we took action to correct this situation.

Management insensitivity is never acceptable, but when it involves minorities, women or the handicapped, it has an especially negative effect on our equal opportunity efforts.

I believe that equal opportunity means giving people a fair chance to prove themselves – giving them the opportunity to excel, to take on high-risk projects and demanding assignments.

Our policy continues to be one of hiring and promoting the most qualified people. But you should be certain that minorities, women and the handicapped compete on an equal basis with everyone else.

Frank T. Cary

Number 1-80:   April 11, 1980

IBM has long enjoyed a reputation for being a good corporate citizen. It has made us welcome in big and small communities alike and gained us the local cooperation every growing business requires. Today, when communities everywhere have high expectations of business and at the same time are concerned about the possible harmful effects of business, good community relations is more important than ever.

Everyone in IBM contributes to community relations, but managers have a special responsibility. Every manager, for example, should encourage maximum use of the Fund for Community Service and other IBM programs to promote employee participation in community affairs.

Beyond that, certain managers have a special responsibility to make sure IBM is well represented in the community. Local management should be alert to community needs and be quick to contribute time, money or expertise, as appropriate. This might mean serving on the local United Way board, running a Junior Achievement company, teaching at a minority training center, organizing a halfway house, or raising funds for a symphony orchestra.

In addition, in every city where we do business, one branch manager has been designated as the focal point for community relations. Although this person is usually from the Data Processing Division, all branch managers in a particular city – no matter what division – share in the responsibility for community relations and should work as a team. When the designated manager, the team leader, needs help from other managers, they should give it promptly and in a spirit of cooperation.

To provide greater support for our community relations efforts, we recently increased significantly the total discretionary fund for our sites. Now, we are increasing the discretionary fund for our branch offices. We are also raising the limits on the amount of money that can be authorized at the various locations.

On the whole, we are doing an effective job. But good community relations requires continuing management attention, and I am asking you to provide it.

Frank T. Cary

Number 2-80: July 14, 1980

Recently, an investment firm issued a report on IBM that contained confidential information about a product still under development. I am certain that this information could have come only from an IBM employee, and we are investigating to determine who is responsible.

When leaks of this kind occur, we all lose. They reveal to our competitors where our R&D effort is concentrated, what products we have in the pipeline, and the direction of our marketing strategy.

The solution to this problem comes in two parts:

- All IBM employees must be told how damaging it can be to discuss sensitive matters about the company with outsiders.
- Strong disciplinary action will be taken against anyone who has misused confidential information, and civil or criminal remedies will be sought where appropriate.

It is clear that some people who specialize in studying IBM are getting information through personal relationships with our employees. This is intolerable.

Some people, including security analysts and the press, have legitimate reasons to ask questions about us. We try to cooperate with them. But we do so in a way that provides safeguards.

The Treasurer's office has the responsibility to represent IBM to the financial community. If you receive inquiries from the press, you should call on information specialists in Communications to help handle the questions.

I expect all IBM managers to make clear to their people the damage that can result from leaks, and their responsibility in keeping IBM matters confidential.

Frank T. Cary

Number 3-80: December 19, 1980

Recently, I have reviewed a number of Open Door appeals
from employees who had been demoted or dismissed. The
managers involved had made big issues out of employment
conditions, such as lateness, when the real issue was unsatisfactory job performance. Even worse, these managers had
prepared a great deal of defensive documentation, apparently
anticipating an Open Door investigation.

Where we find violations of working conditions, we should
counsel employees and take whatever action is appropriate.
But if poor job performance is the issue, then step up to it.
Unsatisfactory performance has always been a valid reason for
demotion or dismissal.

As for documentation, it should be simple and straightforward, covering the major points of commitment and action.
The purpose is to help the employee improve performance,
and not to create a record that condemns the employee and
protects the manager.

The Open Door policy, which guarantees every IBM
employee the right to appeal an unfair management action,
follows naturally from our basic belief in respect for the individual. It has been an effective deterrent to bad management
because managers know their decisions may have to face the
test of an Open Door investigation. Remember, however, that
the test asks not what is the volume of documentation, but
what are the issues, are they relevant, and has the manager
treated the employee fairly.

John R. Opel

Briefings 1-81 through 5-84
1981 – 1984

John R. Opel

Number 1-81:   September 11, 1981

Organizations seem to have an irresistible tendency to codify successful practices in rules, instructions and controls which soon begin to take the place of judgment. When that happens, the result is bureaucracy.

IBM is not immune. Earlier this year, reports from many sources indicated to me that a growing bureaucracy is affecting the performance of our business. In an initial investigation of the reports, we found the following examples – to mention just a few. People were being required to submit receipts for expenditures of as little as 50 cents. Managers were not being reimbursed for such fundamental gestures as sending flowers to hospitalized employees. One study found that a development group had to wait eight weeks and get 31 signatures in order to buy a small piece of equipment needed to work on a critical business problem. People also complained that procedural roadblocks prevent them from getting the IBM equipment needed to do their jobs.

We have taken some immediate steps to introduce more common sense and flexibility in such areas as travel guidelines, employee recognition, reimbursement of expenses and approvals for meetings. We also have taken action to give additional current-line information systems equipment to our people.

This is merely a start. Other initiatives will come. Meantime, corporate staff heads, group executives, and the division presidents are exploring ways to reduce unnecessary controls, rules and approvals in their areas of responsibility.

But such actions alone will not stop the drift toward bureaucracy. We will succeed in that effort only if you managers, at every level of the business, are willing to stand up and fight bureaucracy wherever you find it. Certainly, there are policies, rules and controls that are necessary, but rules should not become a pervasive substitute for human judgment.

If you have all the information to make a decision, *make* it. If some regulation clearly stands in the way of your doing your job, *challenge* it – take it up the line. If you still believe a certain rule is contrary to the best interests of the business, and you can't get a reasonable answer as to why it exists, let me know about it.

You are managers because you've shown you have the judgment to decide what is right. I intend for you also to have the flexibility to *do* what's right.

John R. Opel

Number 2-81: December 1, 1981

As IBMers, we take pride in the fact that we work for a quality company, one that is dedicated to excellence in products, customer service and human relations. The very name IBM, in fact, has always signified quality.

In a recent survey, managers working for major corporations were asked to choose from a list of twenty U.S. companies the ones they believe have a reputation for offering high-quality products or services. IBM was chosen by 82 percent of those surveyed – seven percentage points higher than the second-ranking company.

These are encouraging findings. But reputation is a fragile thing. We can all name companies, or brand names, that have lost their reputations for quality and, in the process, lost customers.

Today, and in the years ahead, we will be called upon to deliver products and services that perform at higher levels of quality than at any time in our history. Moreover, we are operating in an environment that is more competitive – worldwide – than ever before. In addition, many of our competitors are doing an impressive job of stressing quality as a selling point. So, not only do we have to *maintain* our high level of quality, we have to *improve* it if we are to be the quality leader in the future.

We have placed a lot of emphasis on improving quality throughout the business, and it is beginning to show some results. Last spring, I wrote to all employees in *Think* magazine to stress the need for defect-free work in every job as the key to being the best in quality. It's that simple. If each person passes on defect-free work to the next person, the end product will be defect-free. All of the controls and procedures we can imagine can't replace the need for a basic attitude in the minds of all of our people that the quality of their work is of the utmost importance.

To make sure we continue to focus our efforts throughout the company on quality leadership, I have appointed a corporate vice president who will be dedicated to the coordination of our quality programs. At the same time, I have asked each division and subsidiary head to appoint an executive fully dedicated to quality.

These appointments are the beginning of an intensified effort to make sure that everyone places the proper emphasis on quality in his or her job. To be successful, each of you must rededicate yourself to quality and make sure the people reporting to you do the same, that is, do things right the first time.

With each of you producing defect-free work, we will surely maintain our leadership in quality.

John R. Opel

In 1981, we saved more than 60 million dollars as a result of recommendations that employees made through the Suggestion Plan. That's an excellent contribution, but I believe IBMers can do better if we let them... if we, as managers, do our job of rewarding and encouraging IBM employees to bring new ideas to the business.

We recently improved the Suggestion Plan by increasing payouts to employees, but more money is only part of the answer. We can't afford to discourage people from using a program that contributes so much to our business. Yet survey results and complaints to my office show that's been happening.

In one of the worst cases, over an 18-month period, a suggestion was submitted and rejected three times. Each time we responded with weak answers, incomplete evaluations and slow turnaround. The fourth submission was an Open Door. After reviewing the suggestion, we accepted it, and the employee earned an award of more than $20,000 – not because it was an Open Door but because it was a good idea that could and did result in substantial savings to the company.

A recent survey showed that employees increasingly are dissatisfied with both the quality and promptness of Suggestion Plan responses. In another survey, half of the people rated the thoroughness of the investigation and the evaluator's understanding of the suggestion as only fair to poor.

People who submit suggestions have a right to expect a prompt response, but don't move a suggestion along just to get it off your desk. If there's a sound reason for a delay, tell them why, and be sure that a qualified evaluator has thoroughly investigated the idea.

Don't send back an answer that you wouldn't want to receive.

This extra effort is more than a matter of courtesy. The Suggestion Plan is good business, and it deserves your time and attention. We should never be too busy to take a close look at a good idea.

John R. Opel

Number 2-82: September 21, 1982

A recent survey of IBMers in the U.S. reveals several findings about the Open Door program that I think are useful. First, a small but significant proportion of IBM employees used the Open Door program last year to appeal some action by their managers. Second, less than 5 percent of those IBMers appealed directly to my office, while about 70 percent appealed to their manager's manager. Most of the others went to division or personnel management. Similar studies of IBM employees in other countries suggest they respond the same way.

These are good signs. Most IBMers work out their concerns with their immediate managers. When they can't, they're not reluctant to use the Open Door program to appeal to higher levels – whether or not they label the appeal an "Open Door."

In addition, the survey reveals that the more managers and employees understand the program, the more positive their attitudes are about it, and the less likely they are to express concern about the impact an appeal might have on their careers.

How many of the employees surveyed felt they understood the Open Door program very well? Only about one-half. Closely tied to this lack of understanding, some employees – about one in four – felt that management would not treat them fairly in the future if they appealed a decision.

So there's room for improvement and there are several ways you can help strengthen the program:

– As managers, you can encourage confidence in the Open Door program by making sure your employees know what it is, how it works, and the confidential way we handle all appeals. The best time to do this is now. Certainly it should be done long before a problem arises, so that there's mutual trust in the program.

– Once you receive an employee appeal, act promptly. People who appeal a management decision are upset and, like any of us, they want the issue resolved quickly.

- When the appeal ends, forget about it. We will not hold a grudge, and there must be no retribution. That's the greatest fear people have about using the program. As managers, you have to reduce that concern by your example.

In far more cases than not, the Open Door program confirms that IBM managers have superb judgment. At the same time, the program shows that we respect an individual's right to appeal that judgment, and that's the most important point of all.

John R. Opel

Number 1-83: September 27, 1983

In the last few years, IBM has undergone a remarkable transformation. We've changed almost every aspect of our business, from products to organization to marketing and manufacturing techniques.

That's good. Our willingness to change is one reason for our present profitable growth. And we have to be ready for more change in the future.

But, as managers, we have the job of implementing change in a way that helps maintain our full employment practice, which is a natural outgrowth of IBM's belief in respect for the individual.

Recently, it has become clear that in the next several years our employees will require new skills. This change will mean that we must better anticipate our needs for the future and plan the retraining programs that will help employees make this transition.

Remember, full employment is more than the search for new assignments. It's a continuing process that includes hiring the right people in the right numbers, thoughtful career and skills planning, and the implementation of training and retraining programs needed to meet the changes we anticipate.

Higher level managers, because of their broader perspective, play a larger role in this process. But, *each* manager at *every* level is responsible for the full employment of his or her people.

We've had a long tradition of full employment in IBM. You and I must recognize the importance of this practice and do our very best to preserve it.

John R. Opel

Number 2-83: October 18, 1983

An IBMer who traveled extensively used a discount ticket, but billed IBM full fare. He also claimed taxi expenses not incurred.

Another employee's rental car expenses showed excessive mileage. When questioned, the employee admitted to personal mileage. Duplicate charges were also found.

The overwhelming majority of IBMers are scrupulously honest. A few, however, have yielded to the temptation to manipulate expense accounts for personal gain. When fraud has been involved, dismissal has followed. Some of the individuals had a significant number of years with IBM and should have been well aware that there is no room in this company for dishonesty.

These incidents have raised two concerns in my mind. First, that there may be misunderstanding among employees of what constitutes dishonest or unethical behavior. Second, that managers may not be fulfilling their responsibility to manage our assets properly.

I expect all of you to understand the part you play in maintaining IBM's high ethical standards and to act accordingly. That means demonstrating, by personal example, respect for the company's assets. It also means setting a tone for your people by reminding them of their responsibility to the company, not only on the day they read our *Business Conduct Guidelines,* but every day.

Certainly, before you sign an expense account, or any comparable document, read it carefully. If any part of it is unclear, ask for an explanation. Employees will not view this as unreasonable. We have a responsibility to ensure all employees are aware of our expectations regarding all facets of business conduct and to maintain our high standards of personal integrity.

John R. Opel

Number 3-83: December 1, 1983

In a recent review of Open Doors and Speak Ups, I found a few isolated cases of managers who had abused their authority through inappropriate personal behavior. There were instances of profanity and abusive language, sexual harassment, a management team's misconduct in a hotel. These few instances bring up several points all of us must focus on.

First, the company respects the individual's right to privacy, but managers have responsibilities that do not always end at the close of business. Managers often travel on business or are away on temporary assignment, alone or with peers and subordinates. Whatever the circumstance, if their behavior on their own time adversely affects IBM's reputation or their own ability to manage, it's a business problem.

Second, if you have any doubt whether certain behavior is acceptable, apply the "sunshine test." Ask yourself how you would feel if the conduct were exposed to the full light of day and the examination of colleagues you respect. If you are uncomfortable with the answer, you won't need a rule book or a formal business review to tell you what's right.

In some of the cases, higher level managers either were unaware of or ignored these emerging situations until it was too late, compounding the problems. It is essential that upper management be alert, aware, and act promptly when such situations arise.

IBM has a belief in excellence in everything it does, and excellence also is our management standard. Most managers do a fine job of fulfilling their responsibilities – but most is not enough. Each of us must make it a matter of personal responsibility to live up to, and encourage, a high standard of behavior.

John R. Opel

Number 1-84: March 22, 1984

Recently, there have been two instances in which documents originating from a competitor and labeled "Company Private" or "Internal Use Only" have been received within IBM and not reported promptly.

In one case the document was received overseas from an anonymous source, but was not brought to the attention of legal counsel for several weeks. The second instance involved a competitor's confidential product information, which was provided to an IBM branch office by a customer. Again, the information was clearly labeled as confidential, but it was accepted and not reported to legal counsel for several weeks.

During the past few years we have reaffirmed many times that IBM expects its proprietary rights and confidential information to be respected by others. Similarly, IBM intends to treat the proprietary rights and confidential information of others with equal respect. In this regard, IBM employees should not solicit, accept, or use the confidential information of others.

Should such confidential information be offered, it must be refused. If it has already been received or found on our premises it should immediately be turned over to IBM legal counsel.

This is not just a question of protecting business property. It's a matter of right and wrong. Every company is entitled to the rewards of its investment and innovation as manifested in its confidential information. I expect all managers to remind their people of the importance we place on respecting the confidential information and proprietary rights of others.

John R. Opel

Number 2-84: April 25, 1984

One of the most difficult, and most important, responsibilities you face as a manager is dealing fairly and effectively with an employee whose performance is unsatisfactory. In these cases, you have basic obligations to both the employee and IBM.

For many managers, it is not easy to sit face to face with an employee and frankly discuss performance shortcomings. And it is not always obvious what corrective action will put the employee on the path to improved performance. Some managers who want to avoid a confrontation may consider transferring an employee. Other managers may make a halfhearted effort to counsel the employee, hoping that performance will improve by itself over time.

These courses of action are not acceptable in IBM. They waste the company's human resources, risk the company's reputation for excellence, and harm the morale of other employees. They also are unfair to the individual involved. Evasive treatment of a poor performer is a violation of our basic belief in respect for the individual.

If you see an employee struggling with the requirements of the job, don't wait until appraisal time to sit down and talk about it. Delay only aggravates the problem for everyone. Identify the deficiency, have a counseling session, and work out a specific plan to improve performance. Your own manager, perhaps more experienced in handling this kind of problem, can provide help. And I expect him or her to do so. But first, you have to step up to the problem.

When counseling and corrective action fail to produce sufficient improvement, you may have no alternative but to separate an employee from the company.

Some managers fear an Open Door appeal if they do that. But I assure you that if you have been candid with the employee and have given the person every reasonable opportunity to improve, you shouldn't be deterred by the possibility of an Open Door. When performance deficiencies can't be remedied, a separation is usually in the best interest of all concerned.

John R. Opel

Number 3-84: June 7, 1984

Work goes better when morale is high. A team spirit prevails, people are more decisive. That's been my experience and I'm sure it has been yours. We now have strong evidence that good morale is related directly to effective two-way manager-employee communication.

For example, in a recent opinion survey, 96 percent of those who said they had good two-way communication with managers were favorable toward the company as a whole. In another example, almost everyone had a positive attitude about his or her manager – when there was ample two-way communication. On the other hand, almost no one had a favorable view of management when communication was lacking.

There also are survey data showing that 1) face-to-face communication is generally more effective than written or broadcast messages, and 2) employees, as well as managers, want to feel free to initiate a discussion.

Two-way communication cannot be an on-again, off-again event. Managers must create an atmosphere in which everyone senses that at all times the channels are open and the reception is clear. It should be a part of your daily routine, your work style. Otherwise, you'll lose credibility and your people will lose interest.

Good communication is smart management, and it demonstrates IBM's respect for the individual. I think the surveys are telling us clearly that by maintaining a continual, mutual exchange of ideas and information, good managers also boost morale and, thereby, the quality of their employees' work.

John R. Opel

Number 4-84: October 2, 1984

Growing on-the-job use of our own products such as Personal Computers and other workstations creates an opportunity for increased employee productivity. It also creates a new management task that requires your close attention: managing third-party software.

Unlike software used in central computing installations, most PC software products are the intellectual and business property of others and, generally, such software must not be copied. In managing employees who use this third-party software, it is management's responsibility to ensure that the ethical and legal rights of our vendors are upheld.

To help make IBMers aware of required software practices, a brochure entitled *Software Guidelines for PC Users* was recently sent to you for distribution to your employees. This material demonstrates our conviction that IBM must stand for leading-edge ethics as well as leading-edge products.

We respect the rights of those with whom we do business. I expect you to communicate and support these new guidelines in that spirit.

John R. Opel

Number 5-84: December 17, 1984

In a meeting early this year, I spoke to senior management about the tendency of news media to exaggerate when covering IBM – especially regarding our size and competitive behavior.

It's frustrating for all of us to read and hear reports of our actions that we know to be less than factual.

A recent example is the cover story in *Fortune*'s December 10 issue, in which we're accused of "crushing" our rivals, "stifling" innovation, and exploiting our size to ensure success.

My letter to the editor of *Fortune* (see next page) takes issue with several key points in the article. You should feel free to use it as a guide in discussing related topics with employees.

By all means, talk with them about IBM's size and competitive behavior. Remind them of our *Business Conduct Guidelines*, which clearly spell out the standard of behavior expected from every IBM employee. And make it clear that we can't be content merely avoiding unethical conduct; we must avoid even the appearance of it.

You should also remind them that our success does not preclude the success of others. Over the next decade, we expect our industry to grow 15 percent each year – with revenue rising from $230 billion in 1983 to more than $1 trillion in 1993. So, even if we grow as fast as the industry, our competitors can look forward to huge increases in revenue.

IBM also has much to look forward to – not because we're big and overpowering, but because we provide our customers with the products and services they want at prices they can afford.

That's the story *Fortune* didn't tell, but that all of us certainly should – whenever the occasion arises.

Mr. William S. Rukeyser   November 28, 1984
Managing Editor
Fortune Magazine
Time & Life Building
Rockefeller Center
New York, NY 10020

Dear Bill:

Fortune asks the question in its December 10 issue,
"Is IBM Playing Too Tough?" To create the impression that
the answer is "yes," it relies on a menacing cover illustration
and warlike language ("casualty list," "maimed" and "crushed
rivals," "salvos," "adversaries…retreated," etc.). But it fails to
employ the most potent journalistic technique at its command
– the facts.

In doing this, the article ignores many of the very successful companies in the industry that have prospered, ignores a
record of worldwide industry growth, and ignores the benefits
to the consumer of fair and healthy competition.

To make his point, writer Bro Uttal simplistically attributes
Storage Technology's difficulties to what he casually describes
as "a new type" of disk drive from IBM. He fails to say that IBM
introduced an innovative and cost-effective technology break-
through – one that competitors were unable to copy. He fails
to ask the question, as many serious business publications
already have done, of what complex internal factors may have
contributed to the problems of a major enterprise.

At the other end of the scale, Mr. Uttal talks about personal
computer companies being an "endangered species." Far from
it; there are literally hundreds of competitors, and others jump
into this more than $15 billion part of the industry every day.

Your story raises the specter of unfair behavior but never
marshals the facts to support the premise.

Sincerely,

John R. Opel

John R. Opel

John F. Akers

Briefings 1-85 through 4-87
1985 – 1987

John F. Akers

Number 1-85: October 15, 1985

IBM has always been known for the high quality of its management. You've earned a reputation for being professional, energetic and sensitive. There's another trait IBM managers show that really sets you apart. That's the way you approach your work: not just as highly skilled professionals, but as "owners" of a business who know they must take responsibility for every aspect of their jobs.

In no area is this attitude more important than in the way *we run our business.* I'm talking about things like procedures, paperwork, accounting, and controls... all the activities we lump together under the term, "business process." In a large and complex organization like ours, the need is especially great for managers to "own" that process.

Billing and accounts receivable provide good examples of why this is true. If a customer receives an incorrect invoice, IBM may not get paid on time. But that's not all. Correcting it involves telephone time and perhaps a customer visit to figure out what went wrong. Finally, we may have to issue another invoice. When you follow the multiplying effects of poor quality in the business process, you begin to see how much it costs in time... and, most important, in customer goodwill.

We have to do things right the first time. That applies to cutting an invoice, processing a purchase order, or writing a memorandum, just as much as it does to manufacturing a product.

More rules, more regulations, and more staff are not the answer. The only way to improve the quality of our business process is for each manager to take personal responsibility for making the business process work.

John F. Akers

Number 1-86: January 6, 1986

Recently, I had occasion to review the principles which guide IBM. In addition to our three basic beliefs – respect for the individual, service to the customer, and excellence – there are four more IBM principles:

- Managers Must Lead Effectively
- Obligations to Stockholders
- Fair Deal for the Supplier
- IBM Should Be a Good Corporate Citizen

These seven principles have served us well. I find it comforting that despite all the changes in our business, they remain as valid today as when they were established more than two decades ago. However, I think one of them needs to be expanded somewhat to reflect our new environment. And that's: Fair Deal for the Supplier.

When this principle was first spelled out, most of the companies we did business with – except for customers, of course – were suppliers. But today, in addition to suppliers, we have a variety of joint ventures, research partners, and third-party channels of distribution, including independent dealers, VADs, VARs, and OEM contractors. In a sense, each of these business associates is a "supplier" too – a supplier of resources, expertise, or technology that we need to move our business forward. And all of these relationships must be managed with the same care and the same ethical concern that we have traditionally pledged our suppliers.

Therefore, we are changing the wording of this IBM principle to read: "Fair Deal for the Business Associate." Specifically, it means we should:

- Select business associates according to the quality of their products, services, or expertise, their general reliability, and competitiveness.
- Recognize the legitimate interests of both the business associate and IBM when negotiating a contract; administer such contracts in good faith.

– Avoid having business associates become unduly dependent on IBM.

In short, the essence of this principle remains the same. But the new wording reminds us that in today's marketplace we must apply it to a wider variety of business relationships.

John F. Akers

Number 2-86: April 24, 1986

After reviewing the results of our most recent opinion surveys, I am happy to report that overall morale is high. I am not happy to report, however, that at an IBM site where morale was not so good, many employees felt that our attention to people management had eroded significantly.

When I asked site management why this had happened, they told me, with the sort of candor I appreciate, that they simply got too focused on getting product out the door.

Our industry is going through some demanding times. I know you're all very busy meeting our business objectives. In this environment, it's tempting to shortchange our responsibilities to our people. Don't succumb to that temptation.

Remember that our people are operating under the same pressures, and they too are working very hard to meet the same objectives. It's a manager's job to provide balance between the needs of the individual and the needs of the business.

Whatever challenges we face in 1986, we must not cut corners on people management. That includes basics such as timely performance plans and appraisals, recognition, and thoughtful career development. But it also means sensitive, ongoing employee/manager communications.

At the same time we also have to strengthen our efforts to stop doing nonessential work that puts unnecessary demands on our people. We must streamline procedures and organizations. We must apply the "sunset rule" to many of our tasks. In the last few years we've discarded many redundant and unnecessary jobs, reorganized to eliminate layers of management and speed decision making, and reduced travel and meetings to save both money and people's time. We want to stop what is marginally useful so our people can focus their time and attention on what is truly necessary.

People management is every manager's principal responsibility. But the elimination of unnecessary tasks also must be very high on every manager's priority list. We achieve our business objectives not in spite of, but because of, our belief in respect for the individual.

John F. Akers

Number 3-86: June 12, 1986

What is the hallmark of a successful leader? Why do some leaders habitually succeed while others, often pursuing the very same goals with the same ability and power, fail? I think leadership style has a lot to do with it.

A recent column in *Time* magazine made the point well: President Reagan is a successful leader because he trusts his management team enough to give them authority to make decisions. Then he backs them up. That's his leadership style, and it pays off.

"Every week Cabinet officers, agency heads, staff assistants, clerks and G.I.'s take it on the chin for the chief and seem to love it," the magazine observed. "Without the President's unshakable faith that we can...do the job," said one government official, "we would have been destroyed by now."

Harry Truman had the same style. As one of his former Cabinet officers said, Truman "had a deep and sincere loyalty to those working for him. He stood by them from first to last."

I believe this is a valuable lesson not only for government people but for business managers as well. Authority shared is authority multiplied. We extend our vision, strength, and effectiveness when we encourage our people to take responsibility. Our trust in them is repaid in higher morale, greater commitment, and a "take ownership" attitude that transcends and strengthens what we require in performance plans.

Trust is implicit in two of IBM's basic beliefs – respect for the individual and the pursuit of excellence.

We demonstrate the ultimate respect for our people when we trust them enough to delegate to them the authority to make decisions, and then back them up when the going gets tough. This frees them to use their talent, drive, and knowledge creatively, to meet our standards of excellence.

Trust is at the heart of effective leadership.

John F. Akers

Number 4-86: October 22, 1986

IBM's 1986 Retirement Incentive significantly expands the number of employees eligible for retirement and provides them with a strong economic incentive to retire before next July. It significantly improves the options available to many of our people. And therefore, it should be welcome news.

However, there is no way around the fact that we are at the same time encouraging employees to voluntarily conclude their IBM careers and telling them it would be good for the company. To a group as talented, dedicated, and loyal as IBMers are, that could seem like a mixed message.

But it shouldn't. There's really only one message behind the 1986 Retirement Incentive: We must reduce our cost of doing business. One important aspect of this cost reduction is reducing the number of employees on the active payroll, but we're going to do it in a way that maintains our basic belief in respect for the individual.

As a manager, what does this mean to you?

It means you should make certain that all eligible IBMers who report to you fully understand the unique opportunities in this Incentive. Everyone who wants to take advantage of it should be given every encouragement to do so. And, if you are eligible, weigh the Incentive carefully yourself.

However, retirement is, and must remain, a personal decision, completely voluntary. No one should be pressured in any way to retire. And no one who chooses to stay should be managed any differently than before.

All of our people, whether they decide to retire or not, should experience no change whatever in IBM's total commitment to respect for the individual.

John F. Akers

Number 1-87: March 3, 1987

I want to share with you a letter I received from an employee which reaffirms the vitality of IBM's basic belief in respect for the individual.

This employee wrote, "Respecting the individual is not just an ideal... it is a reality I witness daily, a reality which has not been compromised."

The letter is a valuable reminder that, even in demanding times like these, we can successfully balance the needs of people with the needs of the business. We have maintained that balance through difficult periods in the past. We must fight to keep that balance in the face of today's challenges.

Respect for the individual remains key to managing the talented, determined and loyal people who are IBM's true strength. I was touched by another passage in the letter which said: "...there's no sacrifice too great or job too demanding that you could ask of me. And I am not alone, for there are many in our ranks who feel as dedicated... we are willing; we will succeed."

I know managers sometimes feel pulled in different directions as they try to meet both the demands of the business and the people who work for them. Managing this challenge means giving people the opportunity to develop to their full potential; it means recognizing and rewarding good work; it means constant effort to maintain the channels of communication between managers and employees.

Managers who pay close attention to these "people responsibilities" soon realize that they are also fulfilling their responsibilities to the business. For as the comments in that letter illustrate, employees who are valued return value. They see the connection between their own goals and the company's goals, and they are willing to work hard to achieve them.

Our employees recognize that IBM has always been a unique place to work. Our managers, practicing respect for the individual every day, are keeping it that way.

John F. Akers

Number 2-87: May 4, 1987

Two years ago, we began improving our basic business processes. Those processes, which represent a huge investment
of IBM people and resources, enable us to develop, build, sell,
install, and collect payment for our products and services.

You have made many business processes more efficient,
more effective, and more adaptable to the constantly changing needs of our business. For example, reducing unnecessary
engineering changes on products at our plant and lab sites has
saved $100 million companywide. In branch offices, we have
improved response to customer calls with a newly designed
online system. The result: our customers receive faster service,
and we save more than $10 million. Quality efforts such as
these are helping to make IBM a tougher competitor in a
fiercely competitive market.

To make sure this progress continues, it is essential that
each of you reexamine the quality programs in your area.

First, make sure the focus is on improving the processes
that are most critical to our business. Second, question reports
or measurements that seem unnecessary. Third, keep setting
the quality bar higher. Look at every process with a fresh eye
and ask: Is this a competitive way to get the job done? Can we
redesign the process to make it more efficient, more effective?
Or is there simply a better way?

Questions like these result in the highest level of quality –
quality that makes IBM more competitive and more attractive
to customers. That's our aim.

John F. Akers

Number 3-87: July 10, 1987

One of the most basic ways we show respect for the individual is by providing a safe work environment for our employees. To start with, we do that by complying with regulations set by government agencies. By that standard, we do very well. Our Occupational Safety and Health Administration record is one of the best in the electronics industry – or any industry.

But government statistics are never enough when it comes to the welfare of our employees. We cannot assume that yesterday's practices are appropriate for tomorrow's circumstances. Therefore, we set our own, often higher standards and constantly focus the attention of managers and employees on the critically important issues of safety and health.

Because we work on the leading edge of technology, dealing daily with new and changing processes and manufacturing techniques, safety requires constant vigilance. We have to make absolutely certain that the safeguards we put in place are adequate to meet changes. Quite simply, if we are to err, it must always be on the side of safety.

The recently announced comprehensive health study, which we believe will reaffirm the safety of our semiconductor clean room facilities, is one more example of our commitment to safe work environments.

But, most important, the best intentioned corporate practices will fail unless managers personally address safety in their own areas. I want each of you to take a leadership role in health and safety. It makes no difference whether you manage in research and development, manufacturing, marketing, or service: safety is your responsibility.

With your help, IBMers will continue to be not only the best employees but also the safest and healthiest.

John F. Akers

Number 4-87: October 21, 1987

An IBMer recently wrote to me about an incident which surprised and disturbed me. He described an IBM meeting where the hosting managers used vulgar language, including off-color "humor" and other offensive remarks. When I looked into the matter, I found, unfortunately, that the story was true. The offenders are being disciplined.

This type of behavior has not been and will not be tolerated in IBM.

Inappropriate language – including vulgarity and sexual or disparaging ethnic remarks – shows a lack of respect for the people who work with and for us. It is diametrically opposed to respect for the individual. Employees don't respect and don't want to work with managers who use it.

I count on managers to set good examples in both their words and their actions. Almost all of you do just that. It also is your responsibility to counsel employees who use inappropriate language and take disciplinary action when necessary.

I expect and appreciate your support in maintaining appropriate behavior throughout IBM.

Index